THE

MAGIC

TOUCH

BILLY RIGGS

THE MAGIC TOUCH

POSITIVELY EXTRAORDINARY CUSTOMER SERVICE

The Magic Touch
Positively Extraordinary Customer Service

Published by:
Tremendous Leadership
P.O. Box 267
Boiling Springs, PA 17007

717-701-8159   800-233-2665

www.TremendousLeadership.com

ISBN: 978-1-949033-01-4

TABLE OF CONTENTS

Preface 7

Introduction 9

SECTION ONE:
THE OLD WAYS CHALLENGED

Chapter 1
Dazzle Them with Convenience 27

Chapter 2
Dazzle Them with Speed 37

Chapter 3
Dazzle Them with Price. 45

Chapter 4
Dazzle Them with Service 57

Chapter 5
Dazzle Them with Service Recovery. 71

Chapter 6
Dazzle Them with Status .85

Chapter 7
Dazzle Them with Quality 95

Chapter 8
Dazzle Them with Friendliness 105

Chapter 9
Dazzle Them with Relationship 121

Chapter 10
Dazzle Them with Fun. 131

Chapter 11
Dazzle Them with Atmosphere. 141

Chapter 12
Dazzle Them with User-Friendliness 151

SECTION TWO:
THE MAGIC TOUCH

Chapter 13
The Greatest Show on Earth 161

Chapter 14
The Critics Get Their Day 175

Chapter 15
Good Isn't Good Enough 189

About the Author 213

PREFACE

This book is written in such a way that it can be read either by an individual or used as a guide for employees to use in groups. Each of the first twelve chapters is followed by questions that can be posed to your team members to help them interact regarding ways to improve your own customer service. If you employ the book in this manner, you may want to begin by encouraging your group to answer the following questions on paper:

1. Name five businesses with whom you regularly do business.

   a. What do you like about this company?

   b. What might cause you to take your business elsewhere?

   c. Are you a loyal customer, or do you frequent them only out of habit or convenience? Phrased another way, "*How* committed are you to this establishment?" Why?

2. Name a few businesses you or your significant other dread entering or refuse to do business with.

   a. What makes the prospect of doing business there so painful?

   b. What could they do differently that might make people more amenable to going there?

INTRODUCTION

Wow! I was floored. After more than 20 years as a loyal AVIS rent-a-car patron, I was transformed into a Hertz customer in a solitary *magical* moment. It had been my practice to always rent my cars from AVIS. I never even called another company to compare prices. Their service was almost always stellar and, on those rare occasions that they failed to perform flawlessly, they corrected their mistakes immediately. But on this one business trip to deliver a speech on Jekyll Island, Georgia, AVIS was sold out so I had reserved my car with Hertz. Upon my arrival in Jacksonville, Florida airport I walked to the Hertz kiosk but was unable to find my driver's license. I had showed it at the security checkpoint before I got on the plane but didn't have it when I got off. To this day I have no idea what became of it.

But I'm a ridiculous over-preparer. I carried with me a *photocopy* of my license, my passport, the credit card I'd used to make the reservation, my insurance card and my auto registration. "I'm sorry," the girl behind the counter intoned. "Florida law forbids the rental of an automobile to a person who doesn't have their license with them at the time of rental." I asked to talk to a manager, and a polite woman emerged to confirm that she "couldn't rent the President of the United States a car if he didn't have his license physically on him at the time."

I was dazed. Taxi fare would be over $300 roundtrip, a charge I couldn't bill to the client since this was my mistake, not theirs. That's when the manager began to *wow* me.

"We can get you a driver," she offered.

"No thanks," I replied. "If I decide to take a limo I'll check out the options, myself."

"No," she responded. "I mean we can have one of our employees drive you up there."

"But that's a 70 minute drive," I objected.

"I know," she answered. "I live here."

"What will that cost?" I asked warily.

"Nothing," she replied.

I was stunned.

"Can I at least pay you for the car I failed to rent?" I proposed.

"No, I can't rent you a car. It's against the law," she replied.

"Can I pay for the gas?" I inquired, still reeling from the shock of it all.

"No," she insisted.

"Can I pay the person who takes me?" I begged.

"No, it will be an hourly employee already on the clock," she said, sensing I was running out of ammunition.

I launched my final salvo: "Can I *tip* the person who takes me?"

"That's up to you," she surrendered.

Twenty minutes later a nice woman drove up in the car I was unable to rent, helped me load my luggage into the trunk of the car, and drove me 70 minutes to the front door of the Jekyll Island Convention Center for my presentation. I offered her $20 for her time and trouble, but she declined, placing a business card in my hand and a metaphorical cherry atop the whole affair:

"Mr. Riggs," she said with a smile, "if you have any trouble getting back to the airport tomorrow, call us and we'll come get you."

That was *magic*. It was customer service delivered with the style and flair of a Broadway musical:
enchanting, jaw-dropping and unforgettable. That's
what I call "Positively Magical Service," the kind of
goose bump-inducing customer encounter that goes
above and beyond the call of duty. In a competitive market, nothing less will grab your customers'
attention, hold it until they buy, and cause them to
eagerly return in the future. This book is my attempt
to help readers raise the bar from customer service
that merely satisfies, to that which captivates and
enthralls.

A New Way of Thinking

The Magic Touch is the customer experience
reimagined, taken to a whole new level. It is not
merely fast, but blistering. It doesn't just get your
attention; it grabs and holds it. It doesn't merely
make you smile, but laugh out loud. It's not only
pleasantly surprising, but shocking. It creates goose-
bumps, leaves jaws on the floor, raises hairs on the
backs of necks and widens the eyes in disbelief. It
is not merely doing the same old things better than
before (although this is important and will be dis-
cussed at length), but also doing entirely *new* things.
It goes beyond improving your normal customer
interactions to make them better than average by
inventing an innovative approach to the customer
experience.

In order to innovate, one must challenge every existing belief and practice, which requires that we identify and remove any preconceived misconceptions through which we interpret our world. The human brain operates much like a pair of contact lenses. Those who wear them are seldom consciously aware that they are peering through the tiny optical glasses and even less cognizant of the fact that every time they open their eyes the lenses slightly alter every bit of information that enters through the eye gate. In the late 1990's central California was suffering from a serious and prolonged drought. Television newscasts regularly reported on the desperate plight of the farmers in that fertile region, showing scenes of withered crops, brown trees, and dead grass throughout the region. Apparently things were so bad the cows were giving powdered milk! At the height of the drought, I flew to Sacramento, rented a car, and began an hour-long drive south into the San Joaquin Valley for a speaking engagement. To my surprise, the trees were green, the grass lush and verdant. I concluded that the reports of drought had been greatly exaggerated. Then I arrived at my destination and removed my sunglasses! Instantly the greenery was transformed into a sea of dustbowl brown. The real world had not changed; it had been dry and withered all along. But my *perception* of it had been completely wrong because of the green lenses I wore over my eyes. Your mind contains layer after layer of "lenses" that cause you to see and experience a world that is quite different from the one that actually exists. Removing these mental filters is a challenging, but necessary task.

Years ago I vacationed in the San Francisco area and browsed through some of the shops at the legendary Fisherman's Wharf. While there I witnessed a hilarious demonstration of a then newfangled technology known today as a virtual reality game. A very large man was standing in a round booth about the size of a kitchen table, with sensors attached to various parts of his body. He carried a toy gun in each hand and wore a virtual reality visor that covered most of his face. The gathered crowd laughed out loud as this man flailed madly about shooting at enemies no one else could see. Imagine for a moment that an angry, hate-filled stalker had followed this man for days and now lurked in the watching crowd. Observing his quarry completely absorbed in an imaginary world, the stalker could not help but sense a golden opportunity to strike. In this scenario, the man wearing the visor might be bigger, stronger, faster, and smarter than his attacker, but all of those advantages would be more than offset by the fact that the stalker is acting in the real world, while his victim senses something entirely different.

IN A BATTLE, THE ADVANTAGE ALWAYS GOES TO THOSE LIVING IN THE REAL WORLD OVER THOSE LIVING OUT A FANTASY.

The underdog would easily be able to defeat his larger, stronger enemy because, *in a battle, the advantage always goes to those living in the real world over those living out a fantasy.* As long as the game-player wears the visor, his situation is hopeless. During the period of time when his senses perceive a world that is different from reality, he cannot see his enemy to strike back or even to defend himself. His weapons are useless, being designed for virtual enemies, not real ones. However, the moment he removes the visor the playing field is leveled. All of his senses are useful again and his advantage is restored. The man with the visor is a living parable of the human predicament; *he was frantically shooting at imaginary enemies while leaving himself utterly vulnerable to real ones.* When creating a paradigm for exemplary customer service, it is first necessary to remove the visor that blinds us to actual problems while we frantically create imaginary ones that divert our time, energy, and attention.

Almost everyone has seen the 9 dot puzzle. (I realize this is "old hat," but I encourage you *not* to skip over the next several paragraphs under the false assumption that you know what's coming. Trust me; you don't.) The puzzle has been around for 100 years, and I remember experimenting with it as a lad. The challenge is to draw four straight lines without picking up your pencil and manage to connect all nine dots. It's difficult because try as you might it seems impossible to do it in fewer than 5, but this is

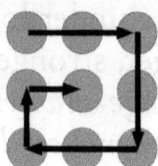

only because your subconscious mind imposes an unspoken rule on the puzzle that was never stipulated or intended.

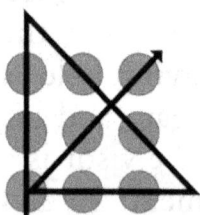

The well-known solution to the nine dot puzzle is displayed on the left. Psychologists say that children have a much easier time with puzzles of this nature, because a baby's brain does not burst into the world already prewired with rules, regulations, restrictions and imaginary barriers. To the contrary, the child's brain is brimming with potentialities. The existence of flying reindeer and tooth fairies and bunnies that transverse the globe with colored eggs in a single night are not merely possibilities, but presumed certainties. From this fact one may infer that creativity is not a learned skill. Rather, it is innate, *then later unlearned.* The pixie dust of original thinking is not scattered on a tiny gifted elite at birth. All of us come into the world fairly coated with it like a powdered donut. But experiences then vacuum it off most of us via externally-imposed rules and systems and by negative people as we age. *This is not a hardware problem, but a software issue.*

More specifically, it is about the operating system of the brain, which has been deposited layer by layer like sedimentary rock over many years based on positive and negative reinforcement received during the formative years. The brainteaser is difficult only because it literally teases the brain. It taunts and defies your efforts because of those mental barriers hidden in the crevices of the brain, the operating system that runs silently in the background filtering and interpreting (often misinterpreting) every bit of data received by our five senses. It is important to note that the conscious mind is never informed of what has been altered, or in what manner it was modified, or by how much. Past experiences cause the adult mind to merely *assume* that coloring outside the lines is prohibited, that extending one's lines beyond the perimeter of the dots is forbidden.

Stated another way, your mind's operating system completely rules out the solution to the puzzle before you even begin to grapple with it! A straightforward and simple problem is thus rendered much more difficult or even impossible. In the 1970s, the nine-dot puzzle began to be used by the Walt Disney™ companies as a metaphor for creative and innovative thinking, and of the necessity to remove all preconceived rules and restrictions from the problem-solving process. This is reportedly the origin of the "think outside the box" meme. *With this foundational set of assumptions in place, we can now use the familiar nine-dot puzzle to take it to some very unfamiliar places.*

If the principle of imaginary and unnecessary rules is true, then, perhaps it would be possible to create an even more efficient way to solve the puzzle. Could all nine dots be connected by *three* straight lines without picking up the pencil? Sure!

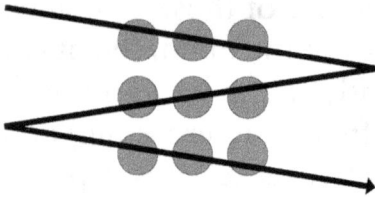

You just need a bigger box! Or, if you prefer, you need to think *farther* outside the box, and you must be willing to relinquish your involuntary impulse to force the line to pass through the *center* of each dot. To begin to think creatively you must remove *all* restrictions on possibilities, even real and insurmountable ones like the law of gravity, and then afterwards dial back or eliminate the ideas that turn out to be actually impossible or illegal. Are there any other imaginary rules that your mental operating system has imposed on the nine dot puzzle that you are unaware of? Perhaps so. Would it be possible to connect all of the dots with only *two* straight lines (again, without picking up your pencil)? As it turns out, yes!

You would just need a pencil the size of a baseball bat. The mere fact that there's no such thing as a pencil that large is a meaningless point for this exercise. Innovative customer service (or innovative *anything*, for that matter)

requires that you begin with a blank piece of paper, devoid of mental limitations. Finally, without the arbitrary restriction on the size of your pencil, you can now connect all nine dots with *one* straight line.

You merely need a pencil the size of a telephone pole. The fact that no such pencil exists is beside the point, because *you could always make one.* You could be the first, should you deem a giant pencil helpful and marketable. That's what creativity is. This is the necessary starting line in the race to dazzle your customers.

The crucial first step in challenging your beliefs is to extract them from your subconscious mind so that you can accurately identify, articulate and evaluate them in hopes of discerning which are true and which are not, and to what degree. Many such beliefs are concealed in your operating system like those mysterious, access-restricted, hidden program files on your computer that are never opened, let alone understood. They limit growth by causing you to live life blinkered, never even seeing the worlds of opportunity that might exist around you.

An acquaintance of mine who grew up in India once told me a story about a Brahman priest who, as he passed through an open-air bazaar on the way to his temple each day, saw a man selling pigeons for sacrifice to Manasa, the serpent goddess. Each of the many birds was tethered to the same single stake by a two-foot length of string, limiting the creatures' motion to perpetually walking in a circle. Round and round they marched continually like the wooden horses on a carousel, day after day. As a member of a religious sect that deeply values all life, the priest felt compassion for the birds and resolved to purchase and free them all. He made payment to the vendor, untied all the strings and attempted to shoo the birds away, expecting them to fly to freedom. Instead, each time he did so, they would merely land a few feet away in a cluster and begin marching in a circle, having been programmed by their limited experience to eschew freedom and return to their imaginary bonds. The birds remind us that it is not enough merely to identify and sever the strings that bind you to old and restrictive customer service strategies; you must also have the courage to fly to a new place and begin to follow altogether different behavior patterns.

The strings that confine and constrain us to old habit patterns lurk in the subconscious mind as neural pathways that are comfortable and well-used. Like rainwater, which always follows the same paths in a downpour and with each storm slightly deepens and widens those channels, your existing thought patterns resist alternate pathways and reinforce themselves every time they are utilized. This is why change often proves so difficult, almost as tedious as forcing water to flow uphill. This explains why people tend to sit in the same pew in church each Sunday and feel out of sorts when someone else takes "their" seats and forces them to plant themselves elsewhere. A neural pathway, reinforced a few times, creates a comforting routine. When you drive to work, your subconscious mind takes over and makes all of the correct turns while your conscious mind might wander somewhere else entirely. Even if you were to change jobs, you might sometimes find yourself heading to the old workplace unintentionally. Once the new route has been established and traveled several times, the old pattern is weakened and a new pathway is created and strengthened until it becomes the new norm. New channels must be forged in the brain, and this takes place only when one is challenged to repeatedly follow an unfamiliar course or travel in a new direction, one that literally electroshocks new connections into existence. Though sometimes difficult, the payoff comes when the new pathways have been fortified to the degree that they become the new norm. The new behavior has become second-nature and the behaviors will then be lived out naturally and without exhausting effort.

Creating a new, dazzling customer service routine might require the combination of dozens of small (or major) changes in your belief system and behavior, not just the addition of one or two new ones. Like all of life, success is a recipe of many items that, when blended and cooked properly, create a taste that lingers in the mouth and the memory long after the food has been digested. New England Patriots superstar quarterback Tom Brady is legendary not merely for his spectacular play, but for continuing to be among the National Football League's most productive players even after turning 40. The average age of an NFL player is 26 and dropping, and the average career length is 3.3 years, according to the NFL Players Association. This makes Brady, in his 18th season as of the writing of this book, even more worthy of the wows he evokes on Sunday afternoons each autumn and winter. But the key to his longevity, if not his success, is his health regimen. No one pays greater attention to diet and exercise. He eats huge quantities of vegetables and fruits, avoids bread, pasta, grains, corn, dairy products, sugar, salty snacks, condiments, sugary drinks, and breakfast cereals. He has elevated stretching to an art form, and lifts weights in a carefully-tailored program that adds to his strength while preventing wear and tear on his frame. In an interview promoting his book on the subject he said, "I can't explain it in 30 seconds. It's a lifestyle. Lifestyle choices. *They're all cumulative. They all add up. And little things, when you stack them on top of each other, are big things.*" [Emphasis mine] Customer service that wows evolves and grows in a similar, incremental way. The many tiny improvements and changes accumulate like so many snowflakes into a huge snowdrift whose kinetic energy may then precipitate a powerful avalanche of productive behaviors.

The cumulative effect of hundreds of choices made each and every day to go the extra inch, if not the extra mile, to return calls promptly, to proofread emails before sending, to study product information to be sure all your answers are accurate, to smile and make eye contact and learn and use customers' names is to turn those many little impressive moments into one huge dazzle in the minds of your patrons. Add to these effects the impact of the new and unexpected benefits you provide your customers and they are certain to be astonished and likely to become your loyal advocates.

Before we can break the strings that bind us to the old ways, we must identify and label them. Almost all human behavior originates in beliefs, whether consciously or unconsciously. Cult members who believe that going to the doctor evidences a lack of faith have been known to let their children die from imminently curable conditions. Fundamentalist Christians have been known to handle poisonous snakes (and die from their bites) because they believed God would protect them. Islamic extremists sometimes strap bombs to their own bodies and detonate in crowded places because they believe they will awaken in Paradise with 6 dozen dark-eyed beauties all their own. Crazy or inadequate beliefs about business and about customer service have similarly resulted in the deaths or anemia of many companies. Identifying them requires that we analyze what customers are seeking when they choose a restaurant, a store, an auto mechanic, a doctor, or any vendor with whom to do business. Twelve factors influence a customer's choices, and each of the beliefs regarding the delivery of these dozen factors must be rigorously analyzed and challenged.

Exercise Questions:

1. Name some ways you might be lying to yourself in your personal life.

2. Name some beliefs you hold about your business or service that you inwardly fear may not be true in the eyes of your customers.

3. Who do you think is closer to the truth, you or your customers? Does it matter?

4. What can you do to help discipline yourself to tell yourself the truth in the future?

SECTION ONE

THE OLD WAYS CHALLENGED

Chapter 1

DAZZLE THEM WITH CONVENIENCE

I shop at The Home Depot at least 2 or 3 times per week. The reason? It's not their variety, prices or service (though I'm happy with all three). It's not their wide aisles or the cheerful greeter who stands by the door to welcome shoppers with a smile and answer their questions. It's not even their generous return policy, though I love that. The reason is quite simple. I live in a small town and it's the only store remotely like it within 15 miles of my house. If, instead of The Home Depot, there stood a Lowe's or Ace Hardware in that same location, I would likely be just as regular a shopper there as I am at The Home Depot. I'm perfectly content with the establishment, so it just doesn't make sense to drive

25 minutes to get a screwdriver or pool chemicals or weed killer from one of their competitors. I can leave my home, buy what I need, and be home in under half-an-hour. In fact, even if I were *unhappy* with them, I would still probably be a regular customer there out of sheer necessity. In that case, I would not really fit the definition of a "loyal customer," though it might look that way to the casual observer. I would instead be a *captive* one, like a person who seems to be happily married but is secretly waiting and hoping to run off with someone (almost anyone?) else once a suitable option becomes available. If a similar business opened nearby, The Home Depot would then in be grave danger of losing anyone who was not truly happy shopping there. Convenience might thus create the *illusion* of a happy customer when the reality is quite different. Give me a competitor just as—or even almost as—convenient and the truth, too late, is realized.

Almost as important as location is the accessibility of a given business. My favorite restaurant in Austin, Texas went out of business about 4 years ago. The food was fabulous, the value was strong, and the location was highly visible on a major highway. Literally thousands (perhaps tens of thousands) of vehicles passed it every day. The establishment was unique, too, an upscale Italian *buffet*, which meant it was possible to get in, start eating your meal within five minutes, and get back to work before the lunch hour was over, having dined on exquisitely prepared gourmet dishes all the while. It was almost impossible to gaze on the buffet spread the first time without whispering, "Wow!" So what went wrong? The restaurant suffered from one major flaw: it was situated in a place where it was very difficult to get to on a one-way frontage road beside a major freeway, mid-block, with no nearby exit ramp. Thus, the myriad of passing cars did not translate into drive-by business because by the time a motorist spied the establishment, it was too late to get off the freeway to visit it. One would have to continue almost a mile down the freeway, exit, make a U-turn, go almost 2 miles, make another U-turn, sit through two traffic lights at busy intersections, and then finally arrive at the location. Just to get off and, after the meal, back on the freeway added about 12 minutes of congested, convoluted driving even if you started within 100 yards of it! You could easily throw a rock out your car window while speeding by and hit the establishment, but you just couldn't get to it. The mere thought of visiting this little gem of an eatery brought many a feeling of, "I don't care how good it is; it's just not worth the hassle." The Home Depot in my community, however, offers no such obstacles. It is totally accessible, standing right at the intersection of two busy roads in the heart of town, with access and egress on both.

Every customer runs a mental cost-benefits analysis prior to a purchase. Price comprises only a portion of the cost calculus, as the convenience factor may add to or subtract from the perceived value of the desired item or service. For example, a plumber who charges $40 per hour but can't come until next Tuesday may thus deliver a lower perceived value than one who charges twice that amount but can come this afternoon. Finding a great deal on the car you want is one thing; finding it 700 miles away is quite another, since the time, money, and effort expended in obtaining it must be factored into the total price. Plus, there's always the risk that once you get there you'll find that the car is not as advertised, and you've wasted time and gas. The price of a commodity or service must, therefore, be calculated as the total impact on the purchaser of obtaining the item, whether monetary, emotional, temporal, or ergonomic. Many a downtown area has fallen into disuse and disrepair because customers must take into account the "cost" of driving all the way there and finding a parking space. Just the anticipation of circling blocks for 15 minutes hoping to turn a corner at just the right moment to see a car vacating a spot causes the customer to think, "It's just not worth the stress." More likely, they just think, "Ughhh!" and dismiss the idea without serious consideration.

One might be tempted to think that the increased amount of leisure time enjoyed by the average American would tend to decrease the negative impact of such inconveniences, but this is not necessarily the case. Along with increased leisure time has come an explosion of options regarding what to do with that extra time. Do I really want to use my leisure time searching for a parking space when I could instead use it to watch television, go to the movies, hear live music at a bar, or dine at a fine restaurant? Am I willing to miss the football game broadcast or my favorite TV program to drive twenty minutes, then walk another six blocks to buy a shirt? I suspect that the net effect of added leisure times versus increased leisure activity options represents a net loss to the seller, though such things are difficult to quantify. Irrespective of how one handles the fuzzy math, however, remains the towering reality that customers demand greater convenience than ever before.

When I was a boy, I remember riding around town with my mother and sisters, wandering from clothing store to grocery store, to toy store, to furniture store in search of a few items to buy from each. Not long after, the first indoor mall in our area was constructed just a mile or so from our home. Now, we could go to a single location to purchase everything except groceries, and those were available across the street. The mall was deemed to be remarkably convenient. But, now, the traditional indoor mall is becoming a relic of the past, because the "convenience" of having all the stores together under one huge roof was surpassed by a new model: having them all in one place on the same level. Note that malls being constructed today are of the often of variety that everything is on ground level and parking is directly in front of each establishment. What was considered amazingly convenient 30 years ago now dredges up visions of wending through huge parking garages, walking to a single entrance, then wandering through hundreds of yards of confusing concourses in search of just the right store(s). These behemoths began to slowly close their doors, or convert into community colleges or megachurches, or lease out to offices or workout facilities instead of retail space. Even the long-term viability of the new outdoor malls is in question. Why? Because their great strength (convenience) competes head to head with the even greater convenience of Walmart and Target. Now, there is no need to park in a multilevel garage and walk hundreds of yards of concourses from Dillard's, to Macy's to Sears to J.C. Penney. There is not even a need to leave the building and walk three doors down as in the modern mall model. One can now drive to a single store to get almost anything needed, so the huge malls are now… *inconvenient*. So, what could be more convenient than your local Walmart? The internet, that's what.

If I desire to purchase a hardware or garden item that I won't need for a few days, I can often find it online in my pajamas at home in ten minutes and it will be sitting on my doorstep in a few days. The convenience of home delivery adds serious value to products purchased online because, after all, time is money. But even online purchases are regularly left uncompleted. A research firm in England called the Baymard Institute reported in 2013 that slightly over two-thirds of online sales are aborted. The study is quite credible because it actually comprised a synthesis of 22 separate studies that had been conducted by others. The *average* of those studies revealed that 67.5% of online shopping carts are left abandoned. One study placed the abandonment rate at over 80%. Many of these lost sales, perhaps one-third according to the studies, are simply the result of people browsing casually (like window shopping) with no intent to purchase, at least for now. There was never much of a chance of closing those sales, anyway. But this still leaves another two-thirds of those potential sales dangling in limbo, never to be completed. Imagine that 2/3 of the shoppers at your local Target abandoned their shopping carts, full of products, in the aisles as the customers who had filled them decided to get back in their cars, drive to Walmart, and start all over again there.

The reason behind such seemingly fickle behavior is the aforementioned cost-benefits analysis, which may change continually throughout the purchase process as new data is received and new factors are added to the equation. The four most common causes of cart abandonment, presented by well over half of those surveyed, were varying expressions of the same phenomenon: unexpected price increases incurred as the purchase process unfolded. While I may find a surprisingly low price for a vacuum cleaner online, the cost steadily rises with each subsequent click of the mouse. The first click reveals the vacuum bags that aren't included in the price but are, of course, essential. The second adds sales tax, which I wasn't expecting because I didn't know the company I was purchasing from is located in my state. Another click offers me a warranty at an additional price. The next click includes shipping, which is extremely high because of the weight of the item. The total cost has now swelled to a price tag that is greater than I would pay for the same item if I purchased it in person at a local store. At this point, I abandon the effort and seek to find a company that doesn't require sales tax or charges less for shipping. Or, I drive to a brick-and-mortar establishment and bring the item home with me.

Most of the remaining complainants cited problems with the vendor's website. It was either too slow, too complicated, or too intrusive (that is, there were too many fields that had to be filled out, or too much personal information was requested). Worse still, almost 40% of respondents said the website timed out or crashed altogether. How many times have you tried to purchase something online and found that the first several attempts failed because an unnamed "required" field was left blank or filled in incorrectly? The final grievance worth noting is that delivery would take too long. Stated another way, after the misleading price complaint, *almost all of the other objections were about convenience issues.* Amazon.com has managed to wash away almost all of these complaints.

Amazon.com removed the price, security, and convenience issues from the equation, and quickly blossomed into one of the most valuable companies in the world. Moreover, being able to order almost *anything* from that one website makes Amazon.com more convenient even than The Home Depot that stands only 2 miles from my front door, or even Walmart. Long gone is the memory of having to drive from store to store (or, thanks to Amazon, even *navigate* from store to store with my computer mouse) to find items of hardware, clothing, medicine, pet food, etc. Amazon has further sped up the purchase process via their "one-click" ordering. The likelihood of leaving a required field empty or having the website time out is now almost zero. Amazon Prime was a further stroke of genius, offering free two-day shipping with your monthly subscription to their music and movie service. And now, in some areas they offer in-home delivery within two hours! Brick-and-mortar outlets' only remaining advantage is the ability to see up-close, feel, listen to (in the case of audio products) and try on (in the case of clothing) the product prior to purchase, and the immediate availability of it.

Exercise Questions:

1. What can you do to make it more convenient for your customers to do business with you?

2. Is there any part of a transaction with you that customers view as a hassle?

3. Is there any point in the purchasing process at which customers might get frustrated and simply walk away?

Chapter 2

DAZZLE THEM
WITH SPEED

A close relative of convenience is the speed at which service is delivered. Like the Tom Cruise character Maverick in *Top Gun*, the customer is shouting to you, "I have a need for speed." Fast food is a relative newcomer to the restaurant industry. Prior to 1960, virtually all food-service establishments were built on the model of a waiter or waitress walking to your table (or roller skating to your car, in the classic drive-ins), describing the specials of the day, taking your order, cooking your food, and ultimately bringing it to you. "Fast food" meant shaving a few seconds or minutes off of the routine. A *really* streamlined operation could turn the food around in 15 minutes, but this required rare coordination, fast communication, and thorough training. The very idea of a drive-through window would have elicited blank stares, for who wanted to sit in their idling car, creeping forward in line one vehicle at a time for perhaps half-an-hour waiting to order (all the while inhaling carbon monoxide), then wait *another* 20 minutes for their meal to be cooked and handed to them through the car window to eat in their laps? Then the paradigm shifted dramatically.

The McDonald brothers of San Bernardino, California invented and pioneered the "Speedy System" of serving burgers, fries, milk shakes and soft drinks at unheard of speeds back in the 1950s. The kitchen was laid out carefully to mass produce a limited number of menu items continually, generating finished burgers as fast as customers could order them. The food was wrapped in paper that could be used to handle the food and then discarded later. Utensils were plastic for the same reason. Drinks were served in paper cups with disposable lids and straws. The entire meal could be prepared, bagged, and handed to the customer in the time it took to order and pay. It was this incredible speed innovation which eventually made the drive-through feasible. But this meant that the burgers had to be precooked, with the result that sometimes they weren't as fresh as they should be when served. Wendy's then came along and shaved seconds off the McDonalds model, while still managing to serve the food piping hot.

My first visit to a Wendy's took place in Atlanta, Georgia in (I think) December of 1976. I still remember the shock of paying for my customized burger and fries and then realizing they had already prepared and bagged my (quite hot) meal for me before I had even pocketed my change! I was stunned. I was certain there had to be a mistake. I said, "No, I just ordered." They read aloud the exact contents of the bag from my receipt to assure me that it was, indeed, my order. They accomplished this feat by cooking the burgers until *almost* done, then keeping them sizzling at a low temperature until they were ordered. They could then be shoved quickly to the front burner, instantly charred, and placed on an assembly line where two or three people would quickly add the exact toppings I had requested in 30 seconds flat. It was amazing to me! Decades later, Chick-fil-A has elevated fast food to an art form. I routinely pull into a Chick-fil-A parking lot and see literally 20 cars in front of me in the drive through lane(s). Nevertheless, I confidently pull into the back of the line without hesitation, confident that each of these cars will be processed at a rate of about 20 seconds each, and I'll be on my way in under 5 minutes. Customers are now a freed breed that have a need for speed, indeed!

In my own business, as a motivational speaker, I try to respond to phone messages, emails or website inquiries instantaneously, often in under 5 minutes. That's why I'm always stunned when I receive an auto-reply from a vendor I've contacted apparently *bragging* that they "strive to reply to all customer inquiries within two business days." Strive? How does forty-eight hours require "striving?" Perhaps "lounge" would be a better verb to use. Or how about "procrastinate?" Why not send an auto-reply that says, "Face it; you're near the bottom of my priority list, right behind taking my cat to the orthodontist!" Even worse, if my request were made on a Saturday morning, that means they may not respond until Tuesday evening! But it might even be longer than that because they only promised to "strive" to return my call by then, implying they sometimes fail to clear even this ridiculously low bar. This is insane! By the time they return my call or answer my email I'll have long since probably completed my purchase elsewhere, or become so fed up with them that I'll be looking for a new vendor. Every minute you wait provides an opportunity for your competitors to steal the sale or the customer.

"The early bird gets the worm." So goes the old adage. A modern equivalent might be, "The first reply gets the business." Online inquiries should be responded to in seconds whenever possible, for the customer often sends the same inquiry to several of your competitors, too. By simply becoming the first vendor they hear from you will often get their business, and not just because your competitors called after you already closed the sale. It's also because the customer almost certainly said, "Wow!" when you replied so quickly. They now have reason to believe that you will continue to be amazingly responsive to them in the future.

A Harvard Business Review study concluded that, on average, only 37% of companies respond to sales leads within one hour. Almost one-fourth of companies *never respond at all*. And the *average* response time is 42 hours! At times, I'll call an electrician or plumber to come help me at my home. Rather than speaking to a live human being, I'm often shunted to voicemail and leave them a message offering them my business, or at least the opportunity to win it. I'm often surprised by how many of them don't respond for hours, if at all. Why do they pay to market themselves, build websites, purchase ads on the web, and then not respond to the leads generated by all of that effort and expense? Even one-person operations have cell phones, don't they? They should interrupt whatever they are doing (barring emergency, of course) to answer their phones by the third ring, or return such calls within a few minutes, at most!

Many customers interact with potential vendors via social media, or at least attempt to do so. While 90% of companies report responding promptly to such inquiries, only 58% of customers say they ever heard back from the vendor, and the response times were generally counted in hours, not minutes. The Interactive Intelligence Group surveyed customers and found that they rated "a timely response" to be more important to them than efficiency, follow-up, product/service knowledge, professionalism, and the ability to resolve problems in a single interaction. *The Harvard Business Review* study cited earlier discovered that companies that respond to leads within one hour are seven times more likely to have a substantive conversation with a decision maker than those whose response time is greater than one hour. While 700% seems like a shocking statistic, perhaps it shouldn't be. Doesn't it make sense that the first house painter to return my call will reach me on the phone because I'm obviously close to the phone and thinking about my peeling paint? And won't I be glad to receive the call so promptly? And, if I give the first or second caller the contract, am I going to waste my time giving all the details of the job to someone who calls three hours later? Of course not. I'll say, "Thanks for returning my call, but I've already hired someone else."

Anyone who has ever worked as a waiter learns early-on that time easily distorts in the customer's mind. As a living, breathing microcosm of Einstein's Theory of Relativity, the customer's wait time before getting served is sometimes perceived in a manner quite different from reality. A diner who sits at a table and doesn't even make eye contact with an employee for five minutes will often exclaim, "We've been here 15 minutes and no one has even greeted us!" The time between placing an order and receiving the food will also be exaggerated in direct proportion to how hungry the customer is. I was once guilty of this minor offense, myself. I was quite hungry and already a little miffed that our waitress took so long to bring our drinks to the table, so when our food seemed similarly delayed, I beckoned her to the table and said, "We've been waiting 25 minutes for our food!" She promptly glanced at her iPad, delivered a few finger taps, and showed me the screen. "You placed your order 14 minutes ago," she announced triumphantly. I apologized, but the woman had missed the point. I *felt* like it was taking too long, and in the customer's mind this is all that matters. Had she stopped by the table once or twice in the interim to say, "I just checked on your order and it will be out shortly," my impatience would have been averted. Had she greeted us more promptly when we were first seated, or merely raced by saying, "Be with you in three or four minutes," my tendency toward frustration would perhaps not have begun at all. As Einstein quipped when trying to explain his complex theory in layman's terms: "Put your hand on a hot stove for a minute, and it seems like an hour. Sit with a pretty girl for an hour, and it seems like a minute. That's relativity." It's not the amount of time that elapses so much as the emotions the customer experiences during that time. Do they feel that the wait staff is trying their best to take care of them despite the long wait? Or do they feel ignored? Five minutes of the latter is more frustrating than 10 minutes of the former. To make the challenge even greater, customers' expected response time is shrinking.

Electronic communication methods and social media have shortened customers' acceptable wait time. If an email goes six hours without a response, more than three-fourths of customers have moved on to another vendor. The percentage of customers who contact a business through Facebook who abandon a request after the same amount of time is even higher (85%). About two-thirds of people who utilize Twitter to contact a company expect a reply within one hour. Texted inquiries demand an almost immediate response. Contrast this with the customer's willingness to wait a couple of weeks for a response to a written snail-mailed letter just a few decades ago.

Exercise Questions:

1. What can you do to improve your speed?

2. Should you establish a policy to return calls, emails or social media posts within 30 minutes?

3. Should you tell your employees to greet every customer within 5 seconds of entering the building (but without making it sound rote and meaningless)?

4. Should you make certain every product ordered from you is in the mail by the end of the day?

Chapter 3

DAZZLE THEM WITH PRICE

In my experience, Dell computers are no better than other brands. They are far from unique. To the contrary, they are rather ordinary as computers go. Their service is not particularly legendary, nor are they unusually fast. Nevertheless, I've owned several of them. They've managed to stake out a huge corner in the personal computer market because they provide an acceptable product at a low price. By creatively managing his supply chain so that parts arrived in the correct numbers and on the precise days when they were needed, Michael Dell was able to spend less than his competitors did warehousing equipment that might not be used for months. Hence, he was able to offer the same basic product, but for less. While perusing the shelves for laptops, one is likely to do a double-take when confronted with a bare-bones Dell model and say, "Wow. I thought it would cost a lot more than that!"

In 2017, Amazon.com purchased Austin-based grocery giant Whole Foods. They almost immediately implemented a new inventory system called Order To Shelf, abbreviated as OTS, which is fundamentally Jeff Bezos' (founder and CEO of Amazon.com) effort to apply Dell's inventory innovation to groceries. The strategy is for the store to order groceries as the shelves begin to empty, timing the delivery of just enough product to replenish inventory immediately before an item is completely sold out. The result is many more deliveries per day of much smaller quantities of food, groceries that can be removed from the truck and taken directly to shelves without warehousing them in the back of the store. Whether this strategy can be effective with perishables (as opposed to computer parts) is yet to be determined, and its toll on workers who are required to monitor the inventory of hundreds of products constantly, place timely orders, and frantically restock shelves could eventually prove unsustainable. Nevertheless, the principle of finding ways to creatively shave expenses rather than raising prices remains sound.

You Don't Have to Reinvent the Wheel

Likewise, Sam Walton made no attempt to create new products when he founded Walmart. His "innovation" was simply to negotiate lower prices from his suppliers and keep his own overhead low enough to pass the savings on to his customers. Walton's motto was straightforward: "We sell for less." They boast of their "Everyday Low Price" guarantee. Their goal is to have the lowest price anywhere on 80% of the items they sell. Of course, selling for less squeezes margins and pressures others in your business to lower their prices in order to compete with you. The result is a potentially dangerous race to the bottom that renders profitability—or even survival—a challenge. But one need not simply lower prices automatically. Instead, you might offer to match any low price that a customer finds elsewhere.

Best Buy advertises that they will match the price of any identical item found on Amazon.com. All a customer has to do is print the appropriate page from Amazon and bring it to the cash register with the desired item at Best Buy to get the automatic price drop. Target stores announced in September of 2015 that they would aggressively match the prices of all their competitors, including Amazon.com and big-box discounters like Sam's Club and Costco. But they upped the ante by offering to refund the difference in purchase price for up to two weeks *after* you buy. Fry's Electronics has an even more lenient price matching policy, offering to refund 110% of the difference between their price and one found elsewhere on the same item, and customers have up to 30 days to uncover and present the cost differential. Lowe's offers the same price-matching perk when measured against local competitors, then goes a step further by dropping their own price an additional 10%, including sale prices. Amazon.com has even implemented an algorithm that constantly searches the web for lower prices offered by its competitors and automatically matches them.

The key is to find creative ways to squeeze your own overhead to the degree that you can undercut competitors on price without reducing your profits. There are numerous ways to accomplish this.

1. One is to contact the vendors from whom you buy parts, insurance, and/or services and tell them you're thinking about putting out their contracts to the lowest bidder next year. Often they will immediately lower their prices to avoid the possibility of losing your business.

2. Another is to rigorously scrutinize the rates of the companies who provide your phone services, cable, internet, and other IT products. Often, by simply mentioning that you are looking for a lower rate will motivate them to suggest ways to trim unneeded services from your package.

3. Consider moving from traditional phone carriers to web-based servers and such as Skype. Use email, Facebook and Twitter to communicate with clients instead of costly overseas phone calls.

4. Allow your staff to work from home and use the extra space for storage to avoid paying off-site providers to warehouse your stock.

5. Join forces with others in your field to create a co-op that enjoys stronger buying power.

6. Move data storage to the cloud. This obviates the need for expensive hard drives (that will eventually crash, anyway) and back-up systems.

7. Compare the company that processes your credit card sales to see if you are being gouged by hidden fees. If you are (and there's a good chance you are), move to a cheaper provider.

8. Use credit cards that offer helpful advantages. I have about 8 credit cards in my wallet, all of which provide me with free hotel nights, airline frequent flier miles, or cash back. These freebies are used to reduce the cost of my travel when times are lean.

9. Never allow a credit card balance to be carried more than 30 days. The interest rates on them are shockingly high.

10. Ask your vendors if they will give you a discount to pay immediately instead of waiting the full 30 days for the invoice to come due.

11. Be sure to carefully monitor when a given credit card's annual fee will be assessed, and decide in advance whether to cancel the card just before the fee is charged, or if the card's perks outweigh the fee. I have credit cards linked to Marriott and Hyatt guest points, each of which charges an annual fee of about $85. However, each card also offers one free hotel night each year, which more than offsets the fee. My business also carries a credit card linked to United Airlines. The annual fee is a whopping $450, but this cost is more than offset by the membership in their airport lounge, The United Club. Each year, I eat about 100 meals in the club for free, which saves me many hundreds of dollars when compared with what I would pay for those meals in an airport restaurant.

12. Tightly control purchasing. Unless someone is watching purchases closely, you will generally find that all of your faucets are gushing cash. Spend at least one

month carefully recording every cent paid out from your company on a single spreadsheet so that you can determine at a glance if any money is being wasted.

13. Scrutinize every credit card and bank account statement carefully. I recently discovered that an insurance policy I had canceled more than a year ago had never stopped debiting my account monthly for the premium. Once they have your money, it's very hard to get it back.

14. Move into a cheaper building, or sublease unused space.

15. Install programmable thermostats that will greatly reduce heating and air conditioning bills when your building is unoccupied.

16. Buy used machinery, furniture and vehicles whenever possible.

17. Use office space more efficiently. As of 2012, the average office space per employee has dropped 20% since 2000. In some cases, workers can stagger their schedules to share the same workstations.

18. Eliminate redundant operations or departments. Government agencies and large corporations are notorious for this sort of wasted effort and money. For example,

the U.S. Department of Defense has 8 separate agencies tasked with finding and bringing home P.O.W.s and those missing in action. One study concluded that government agencies typically employ 4 or 5 times as many supervisors as would be deemed necessary in a private company. As companies acquire or merge with competitors, the result is often multiple redundancies that could easily go unnoticed because no single individual knows both organizations.

19. Reduce the size of your product. Restaurants are notorious for this. How many times have you picked up a hamburger from a national chain and thought, "Isn't this smaller than last time?" Even the Girl Scouts have reduced the number of Thin Mint, Do-si-do, and Tagalong cookies packaged in the boxes they sell. Moreover, the Lemon Chalet Crème cookies are smaller than before. Yet the price per box has risen steadily for decades.

20. Offer rewards to your employees who suggest effective ways to cut costs. Employees might easily spot cost-saving measures that would be missed by managers, because they work on the front line, sometimes many staff layers remote from senior management. They may easily be

able to point out wasteful expenditures that can be trimmed away without affecting mission-critical services.

Any of the above methods will enable you to keep prices low without affecting your bottom line and without having to lay off personnel.

Raise Your Prices... *Carefully*

Another approach is to find ways to increase your prices without losing customers. There are several ways to achieve this.

1. Throw in extra services or bonuses that will make the customer feel the increased price is justified, or at least acceptable. The purchaser will be getting more product at a higher price, but not quite as much more as the increase might warrant in a strict dollar for dollar accounting.

2. Tack on service fees that will be added on the back end of the sale. For example when you buy a movie ticket online, they generally add about $3 for the convenience of doing so. In a saner world, the online tickets would cost *less* than in-person purchases, because the theater doesn't have to pay extra employees to man their crowded ticket windows. But the convenience fees are now an accepted reality of life.

3. When you raise your prices, offer coupons to your regular customers that will bring the price down to the original level, but only for a limited time. This allows them time to adjust to the higher rate gradually and reduces sticker shock.

4. Increase prices only when the economy is booming. Customers will be less sensitive to higher costs when their revenues are strong.

5. Group products together so that the total price per unit is higher. For example, if you sell twelve rolls of toilet paper for $12, you might reduce the package to eight rolls for $10, a 25 cents per-roll increase.

6. Go after wealthier customers. Begin to target people and companies who are not as cost-conscious as those you now serve.

When I shop in the poorer sections of my current hometown, Austin, Texas, I'm always amazed by how much cheaper everything is there. Prices of gas, groceries (at the *same chains* I normally patronize!), and other goods are noticeably lower there than they are 5 miles to the west. In the richer sections of Austin, prices on almost everything are higher. The assumption (and it is usually a correct one) is that people will normally pay more for goods and services if they have higher incomes, rather than driving a few extra miles to find lower prices on those same items. Pitching your products to wealthier people allows you to charge more for the same items or services. However, providing a lower price is a sure way to make customers think, "Wow. I expected to pay a lot more for that."

Exercise Questions:

1. What can you do to reduce your overhead, and thus the eventual cost to the consumer without lowering your profits?

2. How can you raise your prices without the customer feeling the increase?

Chapter 4

DAZZLE THEM
WITH SERVICE

It is quite possible to provide prompt and friendly service that nevertheless remains unsatisfactory. Even an employee who is cheerful, well-groomed and eager to help can be a liability if he or she is not knowledgeable enough about your products to be of meaningful assistance to a customer. Isn't it maddening to ask a question about the features or uses of a product, only to have the staff member reply (even if with a big smile), "I'm not really sure. Let me go ask my manager." Or to have your phone call placed on hold repeatedly by an employee who knows less about their product, company or warranty than you do? Or, worse, to receive answers to your questions that later turn out to be incorrect?

For this reason, there is no substitute for regular meetings with team members to make certain all are updated on your new products or any added features of old ones. Training must be thorough, continual and repetitive. Do your employees know the answers to every question a customer could reasonably be expected to ask? Are they equipped with tools they may consult quickly for the answers to more difficult questions that might come up? Do you brief them each time a product is updated or revised? Have you made it standard operating procedure to pair newer employees with those who possess greater knowledge so they can learn more about your products and services? Do you allow them to listen in on your phone calls to learn how to better position your company? Do you make product manuals required reading for your sales and service personnel? Do they cross-train with one another so that all bases are covered when someone is absent?

My son is a freshman at the University of Texas, and recently informed us that he would like to move off-campus for his sophomore year. My wife and I visited the leasing office of a housing company that operates several different private dormitories and student apartment buildings just west of the campus, housing a few thousand students. The two young men that helped us on successive days were pleasant, conscientious and helpful. Their leasing office was clean and professional. But they repeatedly (and quite innocently) gave us information that later turned out to be inaccurate, resulting in us signing a lease under our misapprehensions and later having to threaten them with legal action before we could get out of the deal. We were unnecessarily left with a bad taste in our mouths that could have been easily averted had their leasing agents been better informed.

Beyond merely equipping your people with the knowledge base they require, you must also entrust them with the authority to act as needed. Employees who know what they should do, yet do not have the power to help, can be even more aggravating than dealing with those who don't even know where to begin. "Empowering agents" is a popular term I hear tossed around by corporations. The term refers to giving employees the technology, authority and training they need to stay one step ahead of immediate need and emerging trends.

Years ago I flew into the Minneapolis airport in the evening expecting to rent a box truck, pick up some large items that had been sent there days earlier, and drive them three hours to a resort where I was to speak. My program was scheduled for the next morning, and I dreaded driving the large, clumsy vehicle down back roads to the hotel and unloading it in the wee hours. As had been my habit for many years, I had reserved my truck in advance with a well-known rental car company. When I approached their counter in the airport with my reservation number, the polite woman on duty informed me that my vehicle was not actually at the airport, but at a dispatch lot a couple of miles away. This, I knew, was standard procedure. (Storing cargo vehicles at airports was regarded as a security risk due to the large amount of explosives they could hold if rented and returned by a terrorist.) "I just need to call my boss so that she can call the lot and authorize the truck's release to the airport," she informed me. I should mention that this event took place in the days before cell phones or even call-waiting. The boss's phone was busy! For twenty minutes, I watched the poor woman dial the phone over and over again, only to receive a busy signal. Between calls, I asked her, "Won't the manager authorize them to send the truck to the airport?"

"Of course," she replied. "You have a reservation."

"Then why don't *you* call the lot and authorize it?" I asked.

"I don't have the authority to do that," she repeatedly replied, obviously frustrated.

Eventually, the boss answered her phone and authorized the vehicle's release. As I gathered my belongings to go retrieve my truck, the exasperated woman shook her head and said apologetically, "I don't know why they hire smart people and then ask us to behave like idiots." Why didn't the boss trust her clearly-competent employee to make the call authorizing the vehicle's release? The outcome would have been exactly the same (the van would be sent over to the airport), but *much* faster, and I would have arrived at my destination earlier and emerged a far happier customer.

My wife and I used to work out at a fitness club near our home in Austin, Texas. It occupied a large, elegant facility, with the weight room and treadmills on the second floor, adorned with 16 silent television sets beaming their respective audio tracks to various posted FM frequencies. Four of the TVs were always tuned to CNN, but the other 12 generally displayed a variety of channels so each member could tune in the soundtrack from the one of interest to him or her. One Thursday afternoon in March I was there, having deliberately scheduled my workout to coincide with the NCAA Basketball Tournament. However, upon my arrival I saw that all 12 of the non-CNN TVs displayed a cricket match from Sidney, Australia. No one was watching. I walked over to the training desk and asked the teenager there, "Would you please change one of these televisions to CBS so that I can watch March Madness?" The kid's response amused me: "No one but the manager is allowed to change the TV stations."

I shook my head in bemused disbelief and replied, "Okay, where's the manager?"

"This is his day off," came his stunning reply.

I said, "What about the manager on duty?"

"She's downstairs," he replied hesitantly. "You're welcome to go talk to her but I don't think it will help."

I walked to the woman's office and politely asked her to change the station on just one television.

"Oh no," she replied. "The boss is adamant. No one changes the TV channels except the manager."

I became a little sarcastic and jabbed my finger repeatedly in the air as though pushing a button. "Can you do this?" I asked.

She was clearly irked. "Yes, but if I do *this*," she retorted, mimicking my finger-jab, "I'll lose my job!"

What do you now think of the manager who wasn't there that day? Do you imagine him as a powerful, virile leader? Or as an insecure imbecile? Customer service is only at its best when each employee has the training *and* the authority to make good decisions.

I recently came across an accounting firm's employee training manual. The business is called Zen Payroll. I wrote down one sentence that struck me as incredibly forward-thinking and empowering:

If you see something, change something. Every employee has the power and responsibility to make decisions as a literal and figurative owner of the company. You're a steward of our values and an advocate for our customers. As such, you're trusted to point the company toward true North.

This value statement reflects a level of confidence that frees employees to dazzle customers in a manner that inspires them to return again and again.

Let me pose a hypothetical encounter between a mythical company we'll call Acme Widgets and three generic types of customers. Which of the following theoretical customers is the most likely to return and buy another Acme widget in the future?

1. Customer A ("Anne") has an altogether pleasant experience doing business with Acme and goes home happy.

2. Customer B ("Bob") endures an unsatisfactory experience with Acme, a product, or an employee, but takes the time to explain his frustration to a staff member or manager. The situation is then resolved to his satisfaction, and he leaves happy.

3. Customer C ("Connie") suffers the same negative encounter that Bob did, but chooses not to complain. She says nothing and leaves angry.

In this artificial, but typical scenario, the one most likely to return next time a widget is needed is Customer B, Bob. Let's explore them one at a time.

Anne received good service and carries, statistically speaking, a 60% chance of becoming a repeat customer. Connie, by contrast, was offended or unhappy with Acme but never complained. She left frustrated and as a result the widget makers have only a 9% chance of selling to her again. Worse still is the fact that she will, on average, tell 9 other people how unhappy she was with the company. She's so upset that when she gets in her car she immediately calls her mother to vent her frustration. At next weekend's dinner party the subject of widgets comes up and she interjects, "Well when you need a widget let me tell you where *not* to go." For months she repeats the story whenever it can be rammed into a conversation. The carnage may be widespread and lasting. Not only will she almost certainly not buy from Acme again, her friends, relatives, and neighbors are unlikely to darken their doors (or type in their URL online) in the first place. But things could have gone much differently.

Bob (Customer B), who took the time to explain and vent his frustration is even more likely to be a repeat customer than Anne is, with a 70% return rate. It seems counter-intuitive that someone who received unsatisfactory service would be more likely to return than the person who felt they were treated well from the start, but on closer inspection this should make perfect sense. Why? Because Bob leaves the store with more information than Anne did, which results in a greater level of trust.

If you were to go to Ace Hardware to buy a hammer and the transaction were to go smoothly, you would leave with only one bit of data: you would know what happens when everything goes right. You are now confident that when there are no hiccups, you will leave Ace Hardware happy and with your desired item. (But isn't that true everywhere?) However, many important questions would remain unanswered: How *often* do things go this smoothly? Almost always? Or was this just a one-time fluke? And what would have happened if I couldn't find anyone to help me? Or if I had been helped by a different employee who wasn't as well-trained, or good-humored? What if the marked price didn't match the scanned one? Would they give me the lower price or demand the higher one? What would they do if the hammer were to break the first time I were to use it? Or the fifth? Or the seventeenth? Would they give me my money back or interrogate me about how I used it? How will they respond if I don't use it for a couple of months, *then* it breaks the first time I hit a nail with it? All Anne can tell herself is, "So far, so good." That's all she has to hold onto.

However, suppose I instead try to purchase a hammer at Ace Hardware but an incompetent clerk can't get the register to work. What should have been a straightforward transaction instead takes 10 minutes. Three different times the sale is rung up at a price higher than the one I'm supposed to pay. Then, the cashier doesn't know how to get the credit card machine to work. Eventually, I become so frustrated that I ask to speak to a manager, who listens carefully to my complaint, apologizes sincerely, straightens out the sale promptly, and gives me a coupon for 20% off on my next visit. Now, I leave with *two* pieces of information:

1. What happens when things go right: I leave happy with my item, and

2. What happens when things go wrong: I leave happy with my item *and a coupon.*

This explains why Bob enjoys a greater level of comfort when doing business with Acme than Anne does. He can rest assured that they have a history of treating customers fairly, so he's more likely to return. The most amazing statistic related to our mythical scenario is the studies indicate that if the first employee a customer complains to solves the problem immediately (that is, doesn't refer the issue to a manager, make you fill out paperwork, or call an 800 number), the return rate approaches 95%!!! This figure represents near-perfection, as the other 5% probably died or moved away. But there is one caveat that must be mentioned.

If Acme Widgets or Ace Hardware messes up my purchase *every* time I go there, I'll soon give up on them no matter how sincerely they apologize or how well they compensate me for my troubles. The key is to maintain stellar service standards, but stand ready to more than compensate for rare mistakes. When seen in this light, mistakes provide a golden opportunity to leap into action and dazzle the customer, leaving them gasping, "Wow!"

Because a customer that leaves unhappy is not likely to return and is quite likely to deter other potential customers, it is very important that you train your people to watch for any signs of dissatisfaction. They should pay close attention to customers' moods, body language, tone of voice, and facial expressions. If one seems frustrated, they should immediately bring that fact out into the open: "You seem frustrated. Is there something you're unhappy about, because if you tell me what's bothering you we'll definitely try to make that right." Employees should be trained never to allow a customer's frustration to go unexpressed, unexplained, or unacknowledged. I recently got a haircut and was frustrated with my stylist. I repeatedly informed her of what I wanted, but she just wasn't understanding what I was asking of her and she never did get it right. I eventually left with a haircut that I didn't like. Two weeks later I returned and was assigned a different stylist. Before she began, she remarked, "You weren't very happy with your last haircut, were you?" Puzzled, I asked her, "No. How did you know?"

She replied, "I could tell by the tone of your voice last time you were here." I was amazed that she remembered me, let alone could recall my frustration. They welcome over a hundred clients each day served by about half-a-dozen stylists, and I'm not aware that I had even met this lady. But she, as she worked with a different customer in a nearby chair, was aware of my level of dissatisfaction while my own stylist remained clueless. If your customer seems dissatisfied, *say something*. Make it right, for this might be your only opportunity to save a customer before they walk out the door forever.

Recently I and my family ate at a nearby restaurant. We live in a small town and eating establishments are few, so we eat here a couple of times each month. I think it's fine, but, my wife and son don't really care for the place. We each ordered a hamburger and waited a surprisingly long time before they arrived... cold. Not merely not-as-hot as they should have been, but literally cool to the touch, almost as though they'd come out of the refrigerator. It was immediately apparent that the food had been ready long ago, but the waiter had not brought them to us in a timely fashion. I told the waiter about the situation, and he apologized and offered to remake them. However, we didn't want to take the time to wait for a fresh order and declined. The manager of the restaurant just happened to be walking by and overheard our conversation. He stopped and asked, clearly troubled, "Your burgers are cold?"

"Yes," I replied.

"All of them?" he incredulously questioned.

I nodded, as my embarrassed wife and son sought with nonverbal gestures and facial expressions to dissuade me from making any further waves.

The manager walked off shaking his head. A couple of minutes later he came to my table, apologized, and told me that he had found my credit card transaction and refunded it (this was the type of restaurant in which you order and pay for your food at the counter, then wait for it to be delivered to your table). He then brought us a free dessert, as well. I left the restaurant feeling *great* about the establishment, knowing that we had just eaten a $35 meal for nothing. Had the manager not responded as he did, we probably wouldn't be going back to that restaurant again, given my family's disdain for it and my own take-it-or-leave-it attitude. But now, I'm certain I'll be back, and I'll drag my wife and son whenever I can persuade them. This is a beautiful example of "service recovery."

Exercise Questions:

1. How can you improve training to be certain all employees have the information they need to answer questions accurately?

2. Do employees feel they have the authority to solve problems? Why or why not?

3. What nonverbal signals might demonstrate frustration in a customer that should be immediately be addressed?

Chapter 5

DAZZLE THEM WITH
SERVICE RECOVERY

Maintaining high customer service standards is essential to building a strong business. However, everyone knows that human beings are fallible and mistakes will occur. Flights are delayed, deliveries are sent to the wrong addresses, food is overcooked, and appointments get forgotten. Regardless of how adept your IT department is, computers sometimes malfunction or crash. Telephone lines go down temporarily, or power lines are broken by falling trees. No matter how good the chef, some people won't like the food. No one can prevent every possible snafu. However, while mistakes are inevitable, lost customers are not.

The Magic Ratio

In the 1970s Dr. John Gottman and his colleague, Dr. Robert Levenson, conducted a simple study with married couples. They put them in a room and asked them to interact for 15 minutes over a contentious issue that plagued their relationship. By watching this brief conversation, they could predict with 90% accuracy whether the couple would still be married 9 years later. The criterion on which they based their prediction was the ratio between positive and negative interactions during the discussion. If there were at least 5 positive contributions to every 1 negative one, the marriage was predicted to last. If the ratio fell below that threshold, almost-certain divorce loomed. If the conflict were marked by teasing, smiles, active listening and empathy, the marriage could survive the occasional outburst of anger or exasperation. If instead the disagreement was fraught with frowns, clenched jaws, expressions of contempt, and turned backs, the relationship was doomed.

Note that even 4 positive reactions to every 1 negative one was a predictor of failure. In business, the ratio of positive encounters must be *far higher*, for it is much easier and cheaper to change restaurants, stores, lawn services, or insurance companies than it is to switch spouses. Yet, even assuming that the vast majority of the time you provide stellar service, the occasional screw up can actually provide a golden opportunity to increase customer loyalty.

Great businesses are prepared to turn their mistakes into even greater wows than they could ever receive by getting things right every time. This is why you must work diligently to create a strategy for service recovery, a clearly defined response each employee is authorized to enact to win over a disgruntled customer. Service recovery is what you do for a frustrated patron to pull the situation back out of the fire. If you do it well, your customers will become more loyal to you afterwards than they would have been had you done things right to begin with. Market share is increased not by statistics and analytics, but by winning over one customer at a time.

I experienced service recovery years ago at the Atlantis Resort and Casino on Paradise Island, Nassau, Bahamas. The Atlantis is a world class beach resort and casino, plus an aquarium (like Sea World) and theme park (like Wet 'n' Wild), and exceedingly opulent. While I was there I was told that Oprah Winfrey and Michael Jackson both had their own apartments there (though I have been unable to document this). The Atlantis was way too expensive for my blood, but I had been hired to perform there for a convention and the company was picking up the tab for four nights, so I decided to take my wife and baby son along with me. To make a long story short, we missed our connection in Miami and arrived in Nassau after midnight. By the time we had collected our belongings and cleared customs it was about 1:00 AM, and we arrived at the Atlantis about 1:30 in the morning.

For any of you who have ever traveled with a baby, you know how the tot's presence complicates and slows the whole process. Not only did we have all of my magic props and products to sell, plus my business attire, we also had all of our personal luggage, the diaper bag, the stroller, the car seat, the beach toys, etc. Piled together, they filled two entire bell carts. The meeting planner for our convention had booked the conference's block of rooms three huge towers away, so in order to get there we would have to walk through two buildings, cross a courtyard, traverse another building, ride the elevator and proceed down the hallway to our room, requiring about a 12-minute walk.

The bellman pushed one cart while pulling another as we trekked to our room exhausted, all the while struggling to console our crying child. When we finally arrived at our destination the bellman inserted the key in the door, but when he opened it the security chain caught and someone inside screamed, "Get out of my room!" They had checked us into an already-occupied room! We trudged all the way back to the front desk. Nearly half-an-hour later we arrived at our new room. Same story! Then it happened *again*! Three different times they checked us into a room that was already occupied by a terrified guest who probably wouldn't be getting much sleep the rest of the night. We'd been in our hotel for more than an hour in the middle of the night and still didn't have a room. The baby was screaming louder than ever and we were dog-tired and fit to be tied. On the fourth attempt to check in, the manager emerged and apologetically said, "Mr. Riggs, we're so sorry this has happened. We're going to upgrade your room." We thought, "Fine." So the bellman pushed one cart as he pulled the other in the same direction as before, but this time he stopped one bank of elevators sooner. We got on the elevator and the bellman pushed the button for the top floor. My wife and I glanced at each other like, "This might not be so bad." As the elevator doors opened we found ourselves facing our room. It didn't even have a number. It had a *name*. The bellman slid the key into the door and opened it. This time we didn't hear anyone scream. Do you know what we heard? Angels singing! It was beautiful and huge! There was a grand piano in the living room of our suite! Do we play the piano? You've missed the point. There was a grand piano in the living room of our suite! Our son had his own bedroom at the far end. Now, at this point were we *upset* with the Atlantis? Of course not! At three o'clock in the morning we were high-fiving each other! We were thinking, "If this had happened one more time we would own the hotel!" And for five days and four nights we lived like Oprah!

Now, more than 15 years later, when we see those Atlantis Bahamas commercials appear on TV, we don't scowl or grumble, "Can you believe those morons checked us into the wrong room three times?!?" On the contrary, we smile dreamily, look at each other and say, "Do you remember that room? We'll never have a room like that again in our lives." Instead of being critics who regale our friends with the tale of Atlantis' incompetence, we relish any opportunity to revel in the glitter and glory of the place. Had the manager not sought to overcompensate us for our trouble, we would most certainly have told the horror tale over and over again to dozens of our friends. As a motivational speaker, I might have told it to fifty thousand people! Instead, I've recounted the story of Atlantis' recovery to hundreds of audiences, effectively buying them the kind of advertising that cannot be purchased with dollars. That's service recovery.

As mentioned earlier, I'm a loyal AVIS rent-a-car customer (save that one brief fling with Hertz mentioned earlier. I eventually returned to AVIS because the good people at Hertz failed to capitalize on their window of opportunity.) One of the reasons I remain so passionate about the company is how they mobilize so quickly to compensate when one of their rare mistakes occurs. As I drove out of the AVIS lot at an airport a couple of years ago, I noticed that the gas tank wasn't quite full. However, the shortfall was so minor (I estimated that it was probably only a gallon or two below full) that I chose not to return to the lot or even call to report it to their customer service department. When I returned the vehicle the following day, I casually mentioned to the lady who checked my car in, just for her information, that they should probably check the gas tank levels a little more carefully before placing them back on the lot for the next customer. She immediately apologized for the shortage, punched a few buttons on her mobile device, and in seconds it had printed out a coupon for $30 off on my next rental. Now I wish all my car rentals were a gallon or two short!

On another occasion, I had reserved an AVIS vehicle for a one-way rental, which often costs much more than the normal practice of returning it to the same lot from which it was picked up. I had been pleasantly surprised when I booked the trip online to see that the price was listed as only $69. However, when I returned the car I was handed a receipt for over $200! I immediately complained and showed the AVIS attendant my rental agreement with $69 prominently displayed as the rental rate. The nice lady then pointed out the fine print below which read, "Additional charge of 25 cents per mile." I was flabbergasted. I had not noticed this before and certainly would have considered other travel options had I known the charge would be so high. I protested that this additional charge should have been printed in bold or large type or highlighted in red. The woman replied, "You're right. That print is just too small. The charge will be $69." A short-sighted analysis might conclude that the employee gave away about $150 in profits. But in the longer —and truer—perspective she further cemented my loyalty to the company. I've spent thousands of dollars renting cars from AVIS, and expect to spend thousands more in the future because they practice service recovery so quickly and so well. The opposite could have happened if this employee had not had the training, judgment and authority to act immediately on behalf of a customer.

I used to book all of my flights (about 75 trips every year) online through Travelocity. I'm a very thrifty person, and never purchase the optional trip insurance. However, about 15 years ago they apparently changed their website so that the system *defaulted* to buying the coverage. Previously, one would have to proactively check the "Yes" box. Now, it was necessary to deliberately *un*click it. I didn't notice the change and mistakenly purchased the insurance on my next airplane ticket without knowing it. When my credit card bill arrived, I noticed the unusual $20 charge and called to inquire about it. When I was informed that it was for trip insurance, I argued that I never intentionally bought the insurance, and suggested to the man on the other end of the line that he should examine my purchase history with the company to confirm I had never once bought it in my hundreds of previous purchases. I insisted that they refund my money, but was emphatically told that I could not cancel insurance after my trip was over. I argued that I was not trying to "cancel the policy" but to point out that I had been tricked into buying it without ever realizing it. (How could insurance be insurance if you never knew you had it?) Long story short, he refused to refund my $20, and I've never even considered booking a flight, car, hotel, or vacation with them since. They could have saved a loyal customer that spent thousands of dollars every year through their site, but they instead threw my business away over twenty dollars.

I suspect that the man who spoke to me on the phone that day was no dummy, and could easily see how foolish it would be to throw away hundreds of dollars in annual commissions from a single customer in order to save a couple of sawbucks, *but he didn't have the authority or means to refund my money on the spot.* There was no system in place to allow smart people to make good decisions and implement them at a moment's notice when the situation called for it. Even if the computer would not allow a refund on a policy for an already-completed trip, the employee should have had the good judgment to assure me that the money would be refunded to me because it was the right and the wise move for the company. He could then find a way to credit me with the purchase price with a manager after I hung up the phone.

Some studies conclude that about half of employees' reactions to complaints actually make the situation worse. It is tempting for staff and managers to write off complainers as unreasonable people who can't be pleased. Or, they simply defend the company's policies or behavior without taking the time to listen to the customer and empathize with them. Or, they sympathize with the customer but tell them, "There's nothing I can do." Some even become angry and belligerent in an attempt to out-argue the patron. It is impossible to win an argument with a customer. The argument, itself, constitutes a loss for the company.

Complaints are a Gift

Because almost every complaint is representative of many (some studies indicate about 26) other customers who experienced the same frustration but decided to inform their friends of their dissatisfaction instead of the company, complaints should be welcomed as a *gift*. Rather than the ruination of your day, they provide a wonderful opportunity to discover factors that are driving your customers away, not only robbing you of repeat business but also dragging down your public reputation. They reveal flaws in the system that may be invisible to employees but loom large in the minds of customers. Complaints often represent the tip of an iceberg that might be delivering fatal blows to your hull beneath the waves, unseen to the oblivious crew whose vantage point includes only the view from its bridge or deck. Remember, your analysis of the quality of your product or service is irrelevant. *Only the customer's opinion matters.* Of all the customer service statistics I have uncovered in my research, perhaps the most frightening and important one is this: acquiring a new customer is anywhere from 5 to 25 times more expensive, (both in financial cost and manpower) than retaining an existing one. Keeping your existing customers happy, then, is the single most important factor in your business' success and long-term viability.

Success also requires that you take the time to *measure* your customers' perceptions of their encounter with your company. It is impossible to know if you are dazzling (or even satisfying, for that matter) your customers unless you create a system that invites, encourages, gathers, and codifies their feedback. Some companies offer a free or discounted product or service in exchange for honest opinions. Others enter those willing to respond to surveys in a sweepstakes, enticing them with the hope of winning a prize. Still others initiate calls to their patrons to ask well-designed questions that will help discern if the customer is being wowed or plowed. One of the greatest challenges faced by those seeking to evaluate the effectiveness of customer service is choosing the right parameters to measure. Often, companies evaluate their service by metrics that are of little relative importance to their customers.

In a bygone era, companies could measure their effectiveness by response times, the quantity of complaints handled, and the number of calls fielded. Employees could be rated by merely analyzing how much paperwork was processed or how many sales were made. But these metrics all overlook the salient issue: what the customer thinks and feels. If your customer's most important issues are feeling cared about and listened to, then all of the other factors may be moot or, worse, misleading. This would be analogous to evaluating an airplane by its current speed while paying no attention to the fact that it's heading in the wrong direction.

Companies who successfully navigate this thorny maze are those who create a single database to compile and analyze data from every customer contact. When a salesperson fields a complaint (or even notices a sign of dissatisfaction in a customer's manner), this information should be available to *everyone* in the company, and in a manner that it will be automatically retrieved by anyone who might have an encounter with that customer in the future. As a company grows, this challenge becomes a larger and more intricate challenge, so the systems that track these bits of data must expand and morph accordingly. A manager's knowledge of an impending cost increase that will affect salespeople must be incorporated into a single database alongside notes from any complaint calls fielded by customer service. In other words, every relevant or useful bit of information must be pulled from each individual source and then pushed to every employee in a form that is not only available but unavoidable. The key is to collect data consistently, enter it in a useable format, and communicate it constantly and seamlessly across all departments.

Exercise Questions:

1. What percentage of positive vs. negative customer interactions do you think must

be maintained in order to retain a customer's loyalty?

2. Does your company meet or exceed that
   threshold?

3. Is there a group of customers you could
   survey to find out if this is, indeed, the
   case?

4. Is there a procedure in place known to all
   employees to solve customer complaints
   immediately?

5. Do employees know what steps they are
   authorized to take in order to satisfy a
   frustrated customer?

Chapter 6

DAZZLE THEM
WITH STATUS

I used to own a Lexus. It's a luxury car pro-
duced by Toyota that varies only slightly from their
far less-expensive Camry. Other than minor alter-
ations to the body of the vehicles they remain fundamentally the same vehicle except for two factors:
1) the sticker price and, 2) the "L" standing proudly
on the hood. I estimate that I paid many thousands
of dollars extra for that little stylized "L." Why?
Because the L brings *cache, baby*! It tells other
people I'm successful, maybe even important. It
screams that I have money (whether I do, or not).
It provides a level of status that the Camry simply
can't. It inspires women to check out the driver. It
gives me a feeling of being important and envied.

It changes other people's opinions of me before we even meet. I'm no longer a nobody when I crawl out of a Lexus. I'm a somebody you would like to meet and befriend. I didn't just purchase a car; I bought the prestige that came with it.

I read an article a few years ago about the hybrid vehicle Prius, another Toyota product. It's a classy, nice-looking vehicle that runs on electricity most of the time. It saves lots of money on gasoline and is easier on the environment than a standard internal combustion engine. But the article revealed the *real* motive behind purchasing that particular car. Most Prius owners weren't attracted to the car by its fuel economy, its stylish appearance, or its ecofriendly nature (though it clearly has all three). Rather, the reason cited most-often by Prius owners for purchasing the vehicle was what it said about *them*. They wanted other people to think of them as individuals who are classy and concerned about the environment. In short, though cheaper cars like the Corolla will get you from point A to B just as well, the Lexus and Prius also confer an admirable status on their drivers.

Starbucks has brilliantly carved out this same niche for itself in the coffee business. It would be quite an easy matter to find a cup of coffee almost anywhere for $1.50, yet there is almost always a much longer line to pay three times that much at Starbucks, because sipping coffee at one of their chichi establishments confers a cool hipness on the customer that guzzling the same cup at Denny's just can't. Drinking coffee at Starbucks implies that you have social status, that you're cutting-edge, that other people want to see you and be seen by you. Imbibing a similar cup of coffee at Shoney's degrades the drinker to the status of a member of the *hoi polloi*, a prole, a working-class stiff, or even a cheapskate. McDonalds' coffee is cheaper, faster, and more convenient than Starbucks'. Their lines move more quickly and no one makes off with your cup of java by mistake as so often happens at the confusing pick-up end of a Starbucks counter. Furthermore, McDonalds serves great breakfasts that Starbucks just can't touch. They serve hotcakes and eggs and sausage and smoothies, while their swankier competitors have a limited selection of scones and muffins. Nevertheless, visiting McDonalds feels slightly embarrassing. It says, "I can't afford Starbucks, and I'm uncool and have no cool or successful friends." If you do run into an acquaintance at McDonalds you wonder if maybe you should avoid eye contact and pretend the chance encounter never took place the way you would if you had crossed paths in K-Mart. I feel that I must manufacture an excuse for buying at McDonalds: "My kid loves the playscape," or "I was in a big hurry this morning." Dunkin' Donuts, likewise, has better food (donuts!) than Starbucks and their coffee tastes better. Consumer Reports consistently rates Dunkin' Donuts and McDonalds coffee higher on blind taste tests than Starbucks'. But visiting Dunkin' Donuts or

McDonald's feels so ordinary, while a trip to Starbucks conjures up images of a European bistro, even though most of their customers have absolutely no idea what a European bistro looks or feels like. No matter. Starbucks doesn't sell coffee any more than Lexus sells automobiles. They both peddle style, status and prestige. They sell a feeling. They trade in *experiences,* not commodities.

Most human behavior is motivated by the desire to enjoy six feelings: security, possession, admiration, belonging, accomplishment, and significance. The first stands, of course, paramount. I will sacrifice all of the others to ensure my survival and to acquire at least a modicum of safety. Therefore, before I pursue any of the others, I must convince myself that chasing those dreams will not cost me too much of my security. Once I am confident of my safety, however, life becomes a quest to fill my soul with all of the others.

Stated another way, security forms the base of Maslow's hierarchy of needs. After I climb beyond the first level, I want five things:

1. to have more than you,

2. to be looked-up-to by you,

3. to be an accepted member of a more respectable society than you and

4. to achieve more than you.

5. If I can obtain a satisfactory measure of these four, I then want to make my life count by doing something that gives life meaning.

These represent the standards by which I compare and contrast myself with others. My sense of happiness and self-worth are not usually proportional to my standard of living, *but by how it measures up against that of my peers*. If I feel happy and content, but then notice that most of my friends seem to have more, be admired more, be more popular, and to have achieved more, I suddenly reevaluate my assessment of my own fortunes. I dismiss my upbeat emotional state as a delusion, a false-positive reading like a test that tells the doctor you have the flu when, in fact, you have only the remnants of your recent flu shot coursing through your veins. "This can't be true happiness," I tell myself. "It must be a Jedi mind trick that life has played on me: *'This isn't the emotion you're looking for.'*"

You ask yourself, "How could these feelings of happiness be real if my friends enjoy more of the things I desire most? What can I do to increase my own status to become equal with or superior to others? Or at least get the *feeling* that I have done so? Or, if all else fails, give *you* the impression that I have?" Well, I could meet a colleague at Starbucks and start catching up right now! I could then post a picture of myself at Starbucks on Facebook so others will be envious. I could tell the person I meet there that I also posted the pic on Instagram, Snap-chat, and Pinterest, thus proving that I am so with-it that I actually know what that is, unlike the hicks and rubes who buy their coffee at Wendy's. I could Tweet that I had a "business" meeting at Starbucks alongside a photo of my White Chocolate Rasp-berry Iced Mocha with cinnamon sprinkles, demon-strating that I am relishing a drink that commoners like you didn't even know existed. One quick trip to Starbucks, and *I'm back, baby!*

Now, imagine yourself posting comparable pho-tos of a similar get-together at Taco Bell. The money you saved, compared with the greater required expenditure at Starbucks, actually improves your financial status and security, albeit infinitesimally. After a trip to the Mexican fast-food establishment I would actually now have slightly more money left-over than I would own after a trip to that snootier establishment. But in my own personal calculus, the reality doesn't matter as much as perception because the difference in price is more than made up for by my sense of increased admiration, belonging and the appearance of accomplishment. I'm not going to Tweet that I drank black coffee at Bob's White-Trash Food Trailer because I know you won't be as likely to admire me for my sensibility (for eat-ing at the cheaper establishment) as you would be to respect me for my stylishness after a trip to Star-bucks. I won't post that I got a great deal on a muf-fin at 7-Eleven because I'm certain you'll be more likely to dismiss me for being cheap than you are to respect me for my level-headedness and practicality. This is a tradeoff that I gladly make, for Starbucks customers are paying for status, not coffee. An equivalent trip to Burger King just won't cut it. To the lower sticker price of Burger King's Croissan-wich, French Toast Sticks, and coffee must be added the social costs of being spotted at a fast-food joint and labeled "cheap." *From* the higher price tag of a scone and Skinny Latte at Starbucks, however, I can *deduct* the benefits of being fashionable. The product, itself, isn't as cheap, tasty or filling, but the fringe benefits offset these shortcomings enough to more than make up for it in total satisfaction. For millions, it's no contest.

The cheapest Rolex watch costs almost three thousand dollars. It tells time the old-fashioned way with separate hands for hours, minutes and seconds. It's small and not even waterproof. I'm not even certain I could read one without putting on my glasses. Amazon.com, however, offers a large multifunction plastic watch that is waterproof up to a depth of 50 meters, includes a big, lighted-on-demand numerical display, a calendar, a wake-up alarm, a stopwatch, and a compass for under $20. Which would you rather have if you were lost in the jungle or stranded on an uninhabited island? There is no question that the plastic watch is more useful in every regard (and for less than 1% of the cost), yet every year people spend many thousands of dollars for Rolex watches that they can't even see! Why? Because other people can see them! The purpose of a Rolex watch is not to tell the time. Your cellular phone does that and you already carry one in your pocket or purse. The purpose of a Rolex is to confer the appearance of importance, status and wealth upon the wearer. The Rolex brand tells others that you possess more, deserve greater respect, belong to an exclusive club, and have achieved more than others.

Marketers of Lexus, Starbucks, and Rolex create the impression that the deepest longings of your heart will be met by simply possessing or using their products. Their brand implies that their customers have money (enough to overpay for coffee, cars, and timepieces) and are socially superior. Lexus and Rolex scream "success" at everyone you pass, while Starbucks declares all who enter her doors to be a part of the in-crowd. Similar feelings are elicited when you throw your Hermes scarf around the neck of your Armani sports jacket. Stride into an Apple store and – *voila!* – you're cool! The fact that the store is open to the public is meaningless. Hipness is bestowed upon you the moment you walk through their doors as though you were entering an exclusive country club. The glow of its trendiness lingers as long as you can keep alive in your friends' memories the knowledge of your visit there. So, you take a selfie inside the store and post it online to memorialize the trip for all eternity. You mention your foray into the Apple Store in conversation whenever you see an opportunity to ram it in, however awkwardly. For a few brief hours or days, you were respected as a member in good standing of an elite and elegant club. Great companies confer status on their customers.

Exercise Questions:

1. Is there a way to make your product or service seem more stylish and classy?

2. Evaluate your website and facilities. Do they convey style and trendiness?

3. Do you use technology that is cutting edge or state of the art? Or do you seem stale and outdated?

Chapter 7

DAZZLE THEM
WITH QUALITY

Price towers over many other factors in the buying process, but no one makes their decision about a product based solely on price. Even price-conscious customers rate the actual sticker price of an item no higher than fourth on their internal ranking of the factors that will determine whether they buy or not. Near the top of the list, whether they are aware of it or not, is quality. As you are reading this book, ask yourself, "Do I drive the cheapest car I could possibly find?" Of course not. There were thousands of cheaper cars out there: cars with no doors, rusted out jalopies, barely-rolling wrecked vehicles. The cheapest new car in America in recent years has been the Nissan

Versa, selling for under $13,000. Yet, they account for less than one half of one percent of all new cars sold in this country. Stated another way, 99.5% of car buyers chose to pay more for a new automobile than they had to. Three decades ago, the cheapest new car on the market was a Yugo, selling brand new for about $3000. But the company went bankrupt in short order as customers chose to pay 5 to 10 times that much (or even more) for a vehicle that they deemed a better buy.

No one reading this book owns, as their primary in-home television set, a 5-inch black and white machine. *No one.* But I saw one on eBay recently for $5, and it comes with a built-in AM/FM radio. And yet you paid hundreds (dare I say thousands?) of dollars for your television set, and it doesn't even have a radio in it! Moreover, no one wears the cheapest clothes they can possibly find. Why? Because they have standards below which they refuse to fall irrespective of price. No one decorates their home with the cheapest furniture or drapes available. In addition to price, they also carefully consider quality.

If you have a leak in your plumbing, you might get the teenager next door to fix it for twenty bucks. But instead, you hire a professional plumber at $80 per hour. No one lives in a tent, let alone a rented one. Instead, you probably paid hundreds of thousands of dollars to purchase your home, when you could live at the Salvation Army for free, and they'd even provide your food at no charge! If you need a $12,000 operation, you don't opt for the veterinarian who offers to do it in his living room for $400. Quality matters deeply, even for those who are not consciously aware of it.

Price-conscious customers may be fooled once by a cut-rate operation, choosing the lowest price over an item of better quality. However, if you make it a priority to stay in contact with the customer whose business was lost to you in favor of a cheaper price, you'll often find a year or two later that they're ready to return to you. My wife used to sell gift baskets to companies who would use them as thank you or holiday gifts for their customers. She regularly sold scores of her elegant baskets to the wife of a local billionaire to distribute to her friends each December. One year, however, the woman opted to go with a cheaper competitor, delivering quite a financial blow to my wife and her employer. A few months later, however, the wealth socialite called my wife to apologize and tell her how embarrassed she had been when she had handed out the competitor's small, skimpy, poorly decorated baskets. They reflected poorly on her. That next year, she returned to my wife's products. By delivering fabulous quality, you also set yourself apart as being unique.

TARGET CUSTOMER BASE

COST-CONSCIOUS   CAPTIVE

↕ VALUE

CLUELESS   NON-EXISTENT

◀ UNIQUENESS ▶

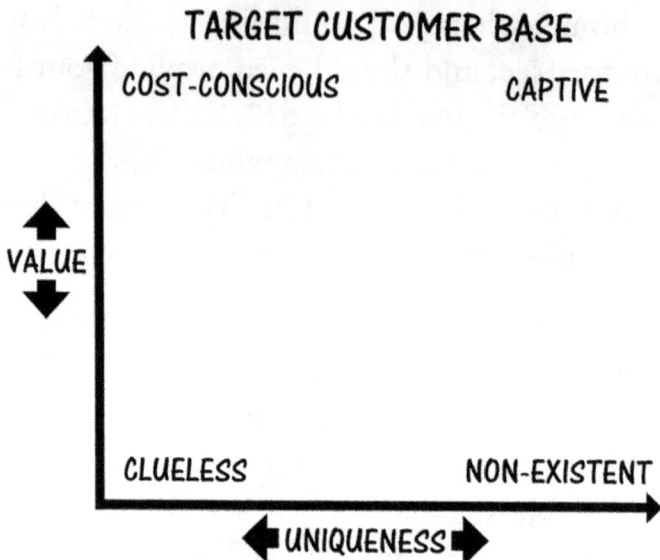

The above graph plots the perceived value (or desirability) of a product or service against its uniqueness. At the top left is a product that is utterly commonplace (that is, not at all unique) but nevertheless represents something people need, want, or value. Groceries, toys, office supplies, and consumer electronics fit into this category. They are must-have products. This is the Walmart corner. Virtually everything Walmart sells can be purchased in other places, but their products are at least items people want and need. Their products are in high demand, but can also be found at Target, Kroger, Dollar General, Walgreens and hundreds of other outlets. Companies who choose to do business in the Walmart corner must outcompete others on price. They may be able to make slight gains over competitors by improving service and convenience, but in most cases the merchants in this corner fight tenaciously to undercut each other on cost. As a result, margins shrink to such tiny levels in this corner that one must create huge sales volumes (as Walmart has done) in order to secure a good profit. A top-left business engages in a perpetual street brawl to win the patronage of **cost-conscious customers.**

In the bottom right corner, you have a product or service that is completely unique but has no value. Among the occupants of this sad corner would be the man who can burp at 110 decibels (a Guinness World Record!), or the guy who eats a series of foods and can then throw up any one of them on demand, or the woman who can simultaneously play two recorders with her nose, one through each nostril. Completely unique, but of no value. I can balance a basketball on my nose. Hardly anyone else can, but this doesn't matter because no one will pay me to demonstrate my rare talent. In fact, most people won't even invest the 20 seconds it would take to watch me do it for free!

Years ago I came up with what I thought was a brilliant idea. I had gone through a divorce that I didn't initiate or want. Not long after, I was walking through a mall that featured piped-in background music in all of its concourses. At that moment, I heard Frank Sinatra's glorious voice belting out his classic song, "You Make Me Feel So Young." I knew the song well but I had a sudden humorous thought when I contrasted the lyrics with the way my ex had made me feel: *she makes me feel like dung*! I like to play with words and rhymes, so I began in the back of my head to write lyrics to that same well-known tune:

You make me feel like dung.
You make me feel there are blues to be sung,
necks to be wrung, and fistfuls of mud to be slung!
And even when I'm 92, I'm gonna curse the day
We said, "I do," 'cause, you make me feel like dung.

I found the exercise so entertaining that I went home and wrote out two full verses so I could have the entire song to sing to myself in the privacy of my own car just for the comic relief it provided. Not long after, I heard an old Elvis tune on the radio and thought, "I could rewrite that one, too." And I did. Over a period of months I rewrote 10 of the world's greatest love songs to my ex! They seemed so funny that I decided to have them recorded. I went to Las Vegas and hired bands and celebrity impersonators to sing my songs so that they sounded exactly like the originals. The song titles were:

1. *You Make Me Feel Like Dung*

2. *Only You (That's All That You Think Of)*

3. *To All the Girls I Could Have Loved*

4. *The Wind Between My Cheeks*

5. *Friends in Law Places*

6. *I'm Gonna Hate You Forever*

7. *Are You Loathsome Tonight?*

8. *You Clog Up My Senses*

9. *You Dried Up My Life*

10. *So Forgettable*

In all, I invested about $30,000 producing and distributing the album. I waited eagerly by the radio (and telephone) as the hosts of a nationally syndicated program talked about my "hilarious" songs and played excerpts of them over the air. They even interviewed me live via phone and allowed me to give out my web address and 800 number and… only two people purchased a copy! As it turns out, there was only one problem with my brilliant idea…. nobody wanted it! It was utterly unique, professionally produced, and—if I do say so myself—quite funny. But there was no demand for it. To the public, it lacked value. It was a bottom-right corner product. Don't make the mistake I did. Don't waste any time or money in this corner searching for customers that don't exist.

The lower left corner of the graph represents products which are in demand and available from many sources, but you sell them at a higher(?!) price than everyone else. Walmart's online store would be an example of "lower-left" thinking. Anything one might purchase at Walmart.com could also be found at one of their local stores at the same price, and many at your local dollar store. However, you must also pay shipping on top of that! The only advantage of the site is home delivery, which you pay for, so there's no uniqueness at all and no increased value. The only customers who shop here are people who are either so clueless or so rich they don't care if they overpay for something they could easily get elsewhere at a lower price. I once had a man pay me $20,000 to do a speech I would have been happy to do for one fourth of that amount. He was so uninformed that he opened the conversation by apologetically stating that he "only" had $20,000 and asked if I would be willing to present to his staff for that amount. *Sure!* People who do business in this bottom left quadrant spend their careers in search of those too clueless to know the value of a product or service or so rich or hurried that they can't be bothered to look for a better price elsewhere.

The top right corner of the graph is where you want to live. Top-right dwellers offer a product that is one-of-a-kind and heavily in demand. Fortune 500 companies pay consultants millions of dollars to tell them to aim for the upper right corner (now, doesn't this book seem like quite a deal to you for under $20?). The upper right-hand corner delivers cache and sizzle that quicken the pulse and make people fork over their money to enjoy the emotional fix they crave. These customers are *captives.* If they want a product, they must buy from you and they must pay what you charge for it because nobody else offers it. If you really want an iPhone (and you do, don't you?), you can't buy one from

Samsung or Motorola. Only Apple makes them. If you long to have that elegantly-shaped "L" on the hood of your car that makes others respect and envy you, you have to get a Lexus, because Ford doesn't make them.

It should be noted that you can sometimes create your own uniqueness from an otherwise common product, just as Starbucks did. I am a "captive" customer of United Airlines. Of course, other airlines can fly me to identical places in similar airplanes for about the same cost, but when I book a flight (which I do scores of times each year) I never even consider using another airline unless forced to do so by my schedule or destination. So how did they transform their "top left" product (an airline seat) into a top right one, a product that only *they* can deliver? They gave me perks for my loyalty that I can't get anywhere else. As a professional illusionist, I check large, heavy bags. I frequently must check 3 bags that all weigh over 50 pounds. Other airlines would charge me up to $250 in extra and overweight checked baggage fees for each one-way trip, costing me several thousand dollars per year. However, United Airlines offers its elite (regular) fliers the privilege of checking 3 bags up to 70 pounds apiece at no additional charge! No other airline offers this perk, to my knowledge, so I fly United almost exclusively. Not only do I fly them regularly, I monitor my usage closely to be certain that I maintain at least Platinum status on that airline. Years ago United Airlines released a memo stating that they were about to rescind the lenient luggage policy and join the other airlines in charging even their top-tier passengers for overweight and extra bags. I wrote them a long letter explaining how their lenient luggage policy was the *only* reason I remained loyal to United, and pointed out how much money they would have to collect in baggage fees from other passengers to make up for the loss of even a single loyal flier like me. I closed the letter by asking them a direct question: "Are you *sure* you want to voluntarily surrender such a powerful customer service advantage?" Shortly thereafter, they announced they would not instate the baggage fees for their elite fliers, after all. I have no way of knowing, but I suspect my letter (perhaps aided by similar ones from other passengers) had something to do with their change of heart.

Exercise Questions:

1. Which corner of the graph does your company fall in?

2. What can be changed to move it toward the upper right corner?

3. Name some ways that you can make your customers captive to you as United Airlines has done to me.

Chapter 8

DAZZLE THEM
WITH FRIENDLINESS

Almost everyone believes they provide friendly service. Hardly anyone says, "We treat our customers like dirt. No wonder they don't come back!" In their own minds, they view themselves as friendly people who are certainly glad when the phone rings or a customer enters the store. The salient issue, however, is not what you think you are projecting, but what the customer perceives. Regardless of how highly you might rank your level of service against that of your competitors, the factor that determines whether a patron returns or not is how he or she rates it. The wise business owner or manager will ignore his own assessment of how well customer service is being rendered and find out from the customers what *they* think. You and your people are biased, and will tend to grade yourselves on the curve, a luxury you cannot count on from outsiders. If anything, they'll be more likely to lean the other direction and downgrade you unfairly.

I used to be a pastor, and noticed that as I consulted with other churches on how to grow their congregations that I never heard anyone admit, "We're not a very friendly church." Why? Because the leaders and staff had been attending there for years and were thus surrounded by friends every Sunday! When they arrive they are greeted by name and welcomed with smiles and hugs. *Of course* people are friendly to their friends! But that doesn't necessarily translate into friendliness toward new attendees (new *customers*, if you will), does it? In fact, the exact opposite often results. This phenomenon often creates a perceived cliquishness that is off-putting to outsiders. Visitors may be greeted warmly when they enter the building, but after that no one speaks to them, invites them to attend next Saturday's potluck or encourages them to join a Sunday School class. The *members* perceive themselves to be friendly and welcoming, but the only factor that really matters is whether *newcomers* find your people friendly, whether in church or in business.

In an oft-quoted study, the American Society of Quality Control concluded that people stop doing business with a company for the following reasons:

1% Die

3% Move away

5% Transfer their business to a friend

9% Are dissatisfied with your product

14% Are dissatisfied with your service

68% left due to an indifferent or rude attitude of an employee

Note that twice as many customers vanished for the final reason *than all the other factors combined!* While most businesses focus resolutely on revenue, expenses, marketing, process, technology and product performance, they often spend little to nothing on customer service training. They assume that their service is fine because they rarely hear any complaints. However, most complaints are not made to the establishment, they are related later to friends, relatives, coworkers and acquaintances. You'll usually never hear the complaint, yourself.

More business is lost by a typical retail company due to employee indifference (let alone rudeness) than anything else. This may take many forms:

1. The teenage employee who surfs the web on a smartphone and doesn't even acknowledge a customer's presence.

2. The adult employee on the phone who never looks up to see if anyone needs help.

3. The semiretired businessperson who feels their new hourly job is beneath them and thus doesn't merit their full engagement.

4. The waiter who never scans the room to see if anyone is trying to get his attention.

5. The staff member who returns a customer's "Thank you" with "Uh-huh."

6. The bored employee who appears disappointed when a customer walks in, as though being interrupted or put-upon.

7. The staff member who rolls his or her eyes at a question.

8. The worker who doesn't smile or make eye contact with patrons.

9. The cashier who is so involved with the customer they are currently serving that they never bother to glance at others in line and say, "Sorry for the delay. I'll be right with you."

But be friendly, cheerful and engaged, and customers will be more likely to return. Employee training is vital if you desire to provide excellent and friendly service. For many people, a friendly and outgoing manner does not come naturally. Rather, for them it comprises a set of skills that must be learned.

Various studies over the past century have attempted to assess how much of success is due to technical knowledge and how much is the result of people skills. The percentages varied widely, but all agreed on their general conclusion that people skills are far more important. Advancement and raises are doled out more on the basis of one's ability to relate well to coworkers and customers than as the result of knowledge and expertise.

In 2009, Google conducted a study called Project Oxygen to determine the most important qualities they should look for when promoting someone to a management position. According to the company's Human Resources Director, Lazlo Bock, they began with the assumption that superior technical knowledge and skills were paramount, especially in the engineering department. What they discovered, however, shocked them. Bock said, "It turns out that that's absolutely the least important thing. It's important, but pales in comparison. Much more important is just making that connection and being accessible." Out of 8 qualities analyzed, technical expertise ranked dead last among the factors that made a manager successful. In order or importance, these are the most critical characteristics and practices of a superior manager:

1. Be a good coach

2. Empower your team and don't micro-manage

3. Express interest in team members' success and personal well-being

4. Be productive and results-oriented

5. Be a good communicator and listen to your team

6. Help your employees with career development

7. Have a clear vision and strategy for the team

8. Have key technical skills so you can help advise the team

This is not to say that knowledge and skills are unimportant, because they certainly are. It is, rather, to point out that one's people skills, attitude, and approach to life are even more vital.

The first step in making the customer feel welcome is to smile. A smile is understood in every language and culture. If you smile, others will almost always smile back at you. It immediately puts the customer at ease. The smile should be warm enough to convey that the customer is valued and wanted. Some employees object to putting a "phony" smile on their faces, but this is to miss the point. A smile isn't phony simply because you may not feel happy all the time any more than not picking your nose in public deceives people into believing your nose isn't clogged. Smiling at customers as genuinely as possible is as much a part of their job description as showing up for work on time. Moreover, a 2006 study conducted at the University of Cardiff in Wales researched the effects of botox injections. They found that when the chemical made it impossible for subjects to frown, they reported being happier than those who were able to freely scowl. The conclusion is that your facial expressions do not merely reflect your mood; they affect it, too. The very act of frowning reinforces your sadness and drives it deeper. Similarly, the act of smiling—whether you currently feel happy or not—actually elevates your mood. You need not fear acting the hypocrite by slapping on a fake smile, because after you do, it will slowly become a genuine one! Like a feedback loop in a public address system, your smile makes you happier, which causes you to smile more, which in turn makes you even happier.

Phone Etiquette

Even if you're only answering the telephone, it is helpful to smile because your positive demeanor is likely to be conveyed in your voice, manner, and cadence. Take care to avoid allowing your personal emotions to affect your tone of voice. If you're angry at a coworker, or frustrated with your boss, or exhausted at the end of a long day, these feelings must be set aside so that your emotions do not leak through the phone lines to your customers. Make sure you include in your initial greeting an identifier that allows the caller to confirm they've reached the right place, and state your name: "Acme Pest Control, this is Jenny." Phone calls should be answered cheerfully and by the third ring. If I have to wait for a phone to ring 15 times before anyone answers, I'll conclude that my call is an unwelcome interruption of someone who has other things they feel pressed to do. If it's answered on the first ring, I assume someone is eager to help me. Make sure that you allow the customer to explain the reason for their call without interrupting them, rather than abruptly interjecting in the middle of their sentence, "Please hold while I transfer you." Wait for the end of a sentence before replying that you need to transfer them. However, it is equally frustrating for a customer to spend 5 minutes explaining their problem and then learn that their call must be transferred to a different department, forcing them to explain it in detail all over again. Once you figure out that a call must be transferred, wait until the end of the next sentence and politely reply, "Mr. Jones, this is not my area of expertise, so rather than making you explain this twice, let me transfer you to Walter right now so we can start helping you right away."

If you must put someone on hold, be sure to tell them how long you expect to be off the line. Customers go crazy listening to the same on-hold music repeated over and over again, having no idea whether the agent has forgotten about them or will return in another 10 minutes, or is just seconds away from picking up again. The polite procedure is to state, "Mrs. Johnson, I'm going to try to reach our supplier on the other line right now to find an answer to your question. It might take 5 minutes for me to reach them. Are you okay to wait on hold that long, or would you prefer that I call you back after I speak with them?" If they choose to remain on hold, but you end up taking longer than 5 minutes, you should immediately jump back on the original call to let the customer know you're still awaiting an answer and offer again to call them back later if they prefer.

Angry Customers

If a customer is angry, don't try to argue with them or tell them to calm down. This sometimes makes people even angrier. Rather, you should sympathize with them by interjecting assuring declarations like, "I can see why that would drive you crazy," or "That sounds terrible." Once they've had the opportunity to vent their anger, then you can start trying to help them see a different point of view by saying, "Can I help you put some perspective on this?" or "May I try to help you see why this might have happened?" Then you can try to solve their problem. This strategy should be employed whether helping customers on the telephone or in person.

Eye Contact

Making and maintaining eye contact is a trickier matter. As a general rule, you should make eye contact with and greet people immediately when they enter your field of vision. Too much eye contact, however, constitutes a social *faux pas*. In a series of field tests described in the *Harvard Business Review*, Dr. Carol Esmark revealed that eye contact made with customers can actually *reduce* sales by up to 37%! Similarly, invading a patron's personal space shrinks business by up to 25%. The general rule is this: *mirror the customer*. If the customer seeks eye contact, match it with a happy smile. If they *avoid* eye contact, you should do the same. Make it your habit to watch their body language from a distance to determine if they want to be assisted or left alone. When I was in college, I worked through my Christmas break in the housewares department of a large department store. I remember one instance in which I asked a woman and her daughter if I could help them. A couple of minutes later, I asked again, and was again told that they were just browsing. Two minutes later, in a genuine attempt to provide "great" service, I asked a third time, but this time the lady was clearly irked and told me firmly, "I told you 'No" and if you won't leave us alone we'll just go to a different store." In my zeal to be of help, I had become a pest because I wasn't reading the customers' body language or even listening to their words. Overly-eager service can actually become as bad as no service at all, actively driving business away.

When it is appropriate, customers should be greeted with a handshake and an obvious desire to help. However, a handshake is counter-productive overkill unless you're selling big ticket items like houses, cars, jewelry, or boats. I don't want a handshake from a clerk when I buy a Snickers bar. This is even truer in our germ-o-phobic climate. Like eye contact, handshakes and eagerness to help can be overdone to the point of becoming an impediment to sales and customer satisfaction, so a balance must be maintained.

If I'm looking for a new car, I don't want to be bothered by a salesperson on the first few lots I visit. I just want to get an idea of what's available and what the sticker prices are. In fact, I usually make a drive-by of a lot to gage whether I can get in and out without being approached by a salesperson before I stop. If there are too many visible salespeople watching every car that passes, I just drive on to the next lot. I don't want to be set upon by a hungry wolf. However, when I'm more settled on what type of car I want to drive and how much I'm willing to pay for it, I drive onto the lot, get out, and look around to try to find someone to help me. The wise salesperson invisibly and carefully observes my body language from inside the showroom to ascertain whether I want to be left alone or if I need someone to guide me and answer my questions. There is another situation in which eye contact repels customers.

When someone is shopping for extremely personal items, it is far better to avoid eye contact other than during your cheerful greeting as a customer walks into the shop. If a Walgreens customer keeps his or her head down and walks to the part of the store that sells adult diapers, don't follow them there to helpfully explain which one absorbs the most!

The exception, of course, is if they stop in the aisle and look around for a clerk. If they do that, you can be certain they're buying the diapers for someone else. But get too close to a dark-haired woman shopping for hair dye that claims to "Cling to stubbornly gray hair," and she'll abandon the purchase and go to another store to buy the same item.

When a customer walks into your establishment (assuming it's a brick and mortar business), it is important that he or she be greeted almost immediately by an employee. While this simple salutation is less critical in a huge store than it is in a Mom and Pop establishment, even massive box stores like Walmart and Home Depot station a cheerful (and, hopefully, knowledgeable) employee right at the entrance to smile and welcome customers into the store. The greeting not only receives the customer in a pleasant manner, but affords him or her the opportunity to ask for the location of their sought-after items. This practice saves the customer an enormous amount of time and frustration when that door-watching staff member can quickly reply, "It's in the far back corner of the store, aisle 17 halfway down on your left at knee-level." If the establishment is not large enough to designate a full time employee to do this specific task, every staff member should make it their practice to greet customers and be available to make eye contact should the customer want to do so. It's maddening to need an employee's assistance and not be able to find one. It's even more frustrating to be within eyesight of three or four employees and be unable to get their attention or catch an eye. One is stocking shelves, another is sweeping, yet another has his back turned while peering down another aisle, and a fourth is looking at the screen of a cell phone, but none is scanning the store searching for a customer in need. Employees should be instructed to glance around every few seconds in search of any customer who might require assistance. Even an employee who is busy helping others should regularly look up, give other customers a quick glance and a reassuring, "Hi, I'll be with you in about three minutes. Can you wait that long? Or can I at least point you in the right direction to browse while I'm helping this gentleman?" Friendliness is critical to achieving service that pleases.

Take Them There

Whenever possible, the best thing an employee can do is to physically escort the customer to the area displaying the item they seek. Few things are as frustrating as to wander down multiple aisles, frustrated because you are unable to locate the product you want, especially after having been sent by an employee who delivered vague directions. Merely pointing toward the item is sometimes misleading, for it is impossible to discern whether the employee is pointing to an item that is 10 feet away or several aisles over. Pointing communicates that the employee has better things to do than to waste time walking with the customer to the sought item. Bizarrely, some customers view pointing as offensive. If you must point, always use two fingers rather than one so that it won't be misinterpreted by the customer. Let's look at another example of customer service in the healthcare field.

The most common patient complaints received by hospitals, according to an article in *U.S. News and World Report* [By Peter Pronovost, Oct. 15, 2015], are:

1. Sleep deprivation from clinicians coming to do tests and draw blood in the middle of the night.

2. Noisy nurses' stations that can interfere with sleep.

3. Personal belongings being lost.

4. Staff not knocking before entering the room, which can be interpreted as a sign of disrespect.

5. Not keeping whiteboards updated. Updated whiteboards allow patients to know who is caring for them. Patients would also appreciate a notebook where they can keep important information and take notes.

6. Lack of clear communication and not updating the patient or family members if the patient's condition changes.

7. Messy rooms where surfaces aren't wiped down, or the bathroom smells.

8. Feeling unengaged in their own care or sensing they are not being listened to.

9. Lack of orientation to the room and hospital. Patients would like to know how to work the television and how to order food.

10. Lack of professionalism from hospital staff, especially when they are on break. (Even while you enjoy your break you are still, in the patient's mind, a representative and reflection of the hospital.)

Note that *not a single one* of the above complaints has anything to do with the quality of healthcare received from doctors or nurses. Instead all of them are about being treated with respect and sensitivity by hospital personnel. Apparently, a flawlessly executed triple bypass heart procedure and prescribing just the right cocktail of drugs to speed recovery wins you few brownie points with patients. This is because the patient has no way of evaluating whether another hospital would have performed the procedure better or worse. Of course, a botched surgery will weigh heavily in the negatives column because the patient will eventually find out about it. But the patient was unconscious during the operation and doesn't understand the nature or dosages of medicines received. Regardless of whether you are a doctor or dentist or real estate agent or plumber or cashier, your customers will judge you first and foremost on your people skills.

Exercise Questions:

1. Do you have in place a procedure for getting feedback from customers regarding their interactions with your people and company?

2. Rate on a scale of one to ten the friendliness of employees who deal directly with customers.

3. Is there a seminar your people can attend or a book they can read to improve in this regard?

4. Do employees make a concerted effort to walk customers to the correct location (whether physically or virtually) to make a purchase?

Chapter 9

DAZZLE THEM WITH RELATIONSHIP

One of the most powerful influences on a customer is their relationship with a company or one of its employees. For many years I was a happy State Farm policyholder. They insured my cars and my home and I was quite satisfied with their service and prices. They handled my claims promptly and professionally. They did *everything* right but I left them, anyway. Why? Because when I got married at the age of 38, it turned out that my new wife's best friend was married to an Allstate agent! The die was cast and I was powerless to do anything about it. Relationship trumps almost every other factor.

Enterprise Rent-A-Car discovered that an existing customer's likelihood of returning in the future leapt by up to 40% when the renter remembered the first name of an employee who served them. Of course, at an airport location this would probably be a meaningless metric. But at their hundreds of neighborhood locations this factor makes all the difference in the world. Customers feel they have an ally, if not a friend that will make sure all goes well. They have an actual person they know to ask for when they phone in or stop by or need a contract amended. The relationship creates a bond of trust that makes the customer feel safe.

The Power of a Handshake

A fascinating study run back in the 70s tested the honesty of people who used a phone booth in Southern California. For those of you too young to know what a phone booth is, it was a public coin-operated telephone located on street corners everywhere that was used by everyone when they were not in their home or office prior to the availability of cellular technology. Just prior to their obsolescence and disappearance from street corners, the going rate for a call was 25 cents, though I remember using them for a dime when I was a lad. Researchers placed a quarter near a public phone to create the impression that a previous caller had left it there by mistake. Most people picked up and pocketed the coin, but upon exiting the booth they were approached by one of the researchers, who would say, "I think I left a quarter in the booth. Did you see it?" The vast majority of those questioned lied so that they could keep the money. (It's sad that so many people would sacrifice their integrity for two bits!) However, when the test was repeated, the researchers made one slight change. He or she would walk up to the exiting caller, shake his or her hand, and ask the same question. Almost every single one acknowledged finding the coin and handed it over! The mere *feeling* of a friendly relationship—even if a momentary and contrived one—made all the difference in the world. Imagine how developing a real relationship with your customers will solidify their trust in your business and their likelihood to return.

The Importance of Connection

My wife and I attended a church in Austin, Texas for three years. We eventually just quit going there and moved elsewhere. Why? It wasn't the sermons or the music (both were excellent). It wasn't the youth program that our son attended (again, topflight). It enjoyed a terrific and accessible location on a major highway with several points of ingress and egress. They provided ample parking surrounding the facility with short or manageable walking distances. We never had a negative experience with a pastor, employee or attendee. The insurmountable problem was the fact that after three years *only one family in the entire church knew our names* or noticed when we weren't there, and we had already known them before we started attending. The fact is, no one cared whether we attended or not. So… we just drifted elsewhere. Relationships are like Velcro to a business, too. They hold customers securely in place.

I'm a very kind person, and way too sensitive to others' feelings for my own good. I have a bank account at a small credit union in my town, and I've long since decided it's not in my best interest to leave my money there. But I haven't moved my money to the large bank across the street for one reason and one reason only. The credit union is small, and I'm afraid I'll hurt the teller's feelings if I close my accounts. And so my money sits there earning nothing. I stay there only because I think they *might* care whether they keep my business or not. It may just be my imagination. They probably wouldn't bat an eyelash or ever give my departure a second thought, but I just can't bring myself to risk it, even if the only consequence is that the teller becomes momentarily sad and forgets the whole experience within an hour.

Have you ever stayed with a barber or hairdresser that doesn't do a good job? All but the most assertive of us have walked away from a salon or barber shop dissatisfied with our haircuts, but we return again and again (until we just can't stand it anymore, or can come up with a sufficient excuse to change) just to avoid hurting the feelings of the stylist. I do the same on a regular basis. I get my hair cut about every 2 weeks at Great Clips™ just a few minutes from my home. It's the type of shop that assigns you the first available stylist when it's your turn. For months, I routinely got stuck with one woman who never did the job correctly. Mine is not hard to cut. I don't have much hair left! But I don't have the heart to walk in and say, "I'd like any stylist except Susie (not her real name)." So what do I do? I have my wife call there before I leave the house. She specifically asks if "Susie" is working today as though she will allow no one else to touch her hair. If she's told, "Yes, Susie is here until 4:00 PM today," my wife says, "Great! Thank you!" And then I wait until 4:15 to show up!!! Why? I just don't want to hurt that woman's feelings. Therefore, I contort my schedule so that I only go when she's not working. Most people don't want to hurt other people, so they sometimes endure bad service in order to be nice… *if* they think anyone will notice they've taken their business elsewhere.

However, if no one knows your name, and wouldn't even know it if you stopped doing business with them, all bets are off. You can leave Walmart and take your business to Target (or vice versa) anonymously, because you don't have a relationship with the cashier. If you can simply disappear and no one will realize you've gone with another company, you'll do so without hesitation when you're dissatisfied. This is why building a relationship with your customer is a critical component of keeping them loyal. If they know you personally, they'll try to give you a few extra chances to get things right. They'll give you the benefit of the doubt whenever possible.

Caring is Everything

One of the best salespeople I've ever known sold cellular phones and plans. Her genius was not product knowledge. In fact, I have no idea whether she knew much about her plans or not. She probably did, but we never got that far in the discussion. I'm not even certain she was a hard worker, though I'm confident she most certainly was. She spent next to nothing on marketing. All of her time was devoted to relationships. She showed up for every wedding, every funeral, every dinner party, every church service, every book club, every chamber of commerce gathering, every garden club, every service organization meeting in town and talked to *everyone*. While there, she pitched in to do far more than her share of the set-up or clean-up. She was cheerful and loving and kind to all. She was genuinely interested in the wellbeing of every person she knew, celebrating their successes and empathizing with their pain. I know her and can confidently say this wasn't an act. She *really* cared about others. People bought cellular plans from her because it was the absolute least they could do for a person who gave so much of her heart and time to them. The prices and features of the plans she offered were secondary. Relationship was paramount. If there were any way possible, people would buy from her and no one else.

People remember doing business with you when at least one of two factors are present: relationship and emotion. You forget any transaction with people you don't know unless it produces an emotion in you. *Any* emotion. Fear, excitement, anger, happiness all imprint an experience in your memory. You easily remember the weddings you attended in which the bride or groom (or both) were dear to you. You forget the ones that joined people you hardly knew. You remember the championship game you won or lost, but forgot the hundreds of games that didn't really produce deep feelings. This memory would become even more vivid if you were a close friend or relative of someone who played that day. For this reason, every customer reaction should strive to establish or deepen a personal bond with them and produce a positive emotions that help sear the memory of the event into the cerebral cortex.

Build Social Capital

Relationships build what marketers refer to as "social capital." Every time you deliver on a promise or do something nice for a customer you are making a deposit in this account. Over a period of months and years you can accumulate enough trust that slip-ups will be quickly forgiven or dismissed as anomalies. Special care must be made, then, to start making "deposits" as soon as possible with a new customer. The account begins with a zero balance, so a negative initial encounter drives you instantly into the red and is likely to make your first date with a given customer your last.

Everyone remembers the anxiety of a first date with a special person that makes your pulse race: the eagerness, the preparation, the double and triple-checking of the state of your wardrobe and grooming. Even anticipated small-talk is imagined and witty comebacks are conceived and mentally rehearsed. Everything must be perfect. You don't want your date to find your appearance or performance "satisfactory." You want to sweep them off their feet, and make them do a double-take when they behold you so immaculately decked-out. You want them to eagerly anticipate coming back to you for more, and banish all of your competitors from their thoughts and hearts. You want to raise goose bumps. You want them to run home and immediately call their best friend to report excitedly on every detail. Apply some of this same thoroughness to your customers and you'll get the idea of what The Magic Touch means.

For this reason, first-time customers must be your top priority. A long-time customer isn't likely to leave you for being less than perfect on occasion, any more than your boyfriend or girlfriend will break up with you for having a stain on your shirt one day. But a first-time customer might be repulsed by it and walk away before they have an opportunity to experience and fall in love with your good qualities. Regard every customer as a bank account and make as many relationship and positive-emotion deposits as you possibly can, as quickly as possible.

Exercise Questions:

1. Have you explained the concept of social capital deposits to your people?

2. How can you make every customer encounter a positive one?

3. What can you do to deepen your relationships with customers?

4. Do you make an effort to call customers by their names?

Chapter 10

DAZZLE THEM
WITH FUN

Companies who are able to transform customer interactions into fun experiences gain a huge advantage over those who don't or can't, because patrons find themselves eagerly anticipating their next opportunity to visit that establishment, purchase that product, or utilize that service. Even better, they bring their friends and relatives back with them in order to share the fun and experience it again vicariously through others' eyes. They also bring up your business in conversation and encourage others to do business with you. Unlimited by the normal course that inspires a customer to patronize a business only when they need to, these companies enjoy the luxury of having customers *want* to come as often as they can. Most companies strive only to ensure that customers have a painless experience, but making customers smile or laugh will elevate a shopping trip from the status of an errand into an *experience*. In this vein, the product is no longer the item or service being sold; it is the experience enjoyed in the process of purchasing it.

Of course, the Disney companies represent the quintessential example of this principle. Families plan years in advance to vacation in Orlando (or Anaheim, Paris, Hong Kong, or Tokyo) and spend thousands of their hard-earned dollars there. Kids eagerly ask their parents, "Can we go this summer?" Disney is the master of The Magic Touch. (They even call it "The Magic Kingdom.") Any entertainment-related company naturally fulfills (or at least aims to fulfill) the fun aspect of customer service. Movie theaters, theme parks, arcades, television stations, parks, etc. are in the business of creating fun. However, one doesn't have to run a water park or video arcade to make spending money something that amuses. Sometimes, a company can create a culture in which buying a shirt or a flight or a meal can be made enjoyable rather than merely satisfying or cost-effective.

It's Fun-Damental

Southwest Airlines is legendary for encouraging flight attendants to turn the boring, boilerplate preflight *spiel* into a stand-up comedy routine.

Romano's Macaroni Grill places crayons and paper on every table, even requiring waiters and waitresses to learn to write their names upside down on the (disposable paper) tablecloth when introducing themselves to diners. They then leave the crayons, thus inviting you to entertain yourself by drawing whatever you like. Cracker Barrel restaurants place a fun puzzle on every table enticing customers to test their skills, thus also making the wait for their food to be served seem shorter. Joe's Crab Shack applies temporary tattoos on children's arms. The Rainforest Café features an entrance beneath a smoking volcano that "erupts" from time to time. Inside, audio-animatronic animals come to life and dance at regular intervals. Hard Rock Café decks its walls with memorabilia from rock and roll legends. The Alamo Drafthouse movie chain runs hilarious videos before the standard previews begin to roll, inviting customers to come early and laugh instead of sitting bored in their seats checking email, or timing their arrival to coincide with the end of the previews of coming attractions. Just for Feet dominated the shoe business in the 1990s by installing a basketball court in every store so that customers could test their shoes before buying them.

P.T. Barnum (of circus fame) remains today one of the greatest marketers of all time. In 1841 he purchased a failing museum on Broadway Street in Manhattan called Scudder's American Museum. The establishment had lost money for three straight years when Barnum acquired it and renamed it

"Barnum's American Museum." He illuminated the building with a green glow. He filled the "museum" with a combination of live animals, scientific exhibits, "freak show" fare, a wax museum, a lecture hall, a flea circuit, novelty acts, and a theater. It housed a beluga whale in a huge tank, a rifle range, an oyster bar, dancing bears, and a trained seal. During the twenty-four years it was open (it burned down in 1865) 38,000,000 tickets were sold, a figure that exceeded the total U.S. population of 32,000,000. Its highest single-day attendance (in a single five-story building) was 15,000, about half the normal daily attendance of Disney's Magic Kingdom, which occupies 90 acres. Within 18 months of purchasing the property, the museum had repaid all of its debts and was making Barnum fabulously wealthy. Why? He was selling fun.

Why People Buy

Other than a few friends who might purchase something from you they don't want or need because they love you, there are only two things people will ever buy from you: solutions and feelings. People buy solutions to their problems. When their kids are hungry, they buy food. When the dishwasher breaks, they hire a repairman or purchase a new one. When they need a package delivered to someone hundreds of miles away, they pay UPS to take it there for them. If a man has to attend a funeral in a distant city, he purchases a plane ticket and rents a car when he arrives. When a woman sees roaches in her pantry, she pays someone to come kill them. When I'm sick, I fork over my money to the doctor. In each case, the problem gets solved. However, no one *wants* to spend their money on such things; they *have* to. But they'd much rather spend their money to produce the feelings all human beings crave.

When I'm bored, I buy a ticket to a movie, play, or concert. I do this because I hope the purchase will change my negative feelings into positive ones. But if the show I attend is bad, I feel I've wasted my money because it didn't improve my mood. It might have solved my problem by filling an unoccupied evening, but it didn't create the sense of escape and wonder I expect from a great production. It didn't thrill me or make me laugh. There was no exhilaration or suspense or empathy created within me. I wasn't expecting to merely purchase a way to kill time; I was anticipating a feeling of *magic*. I wanted to leave the theater with goose bumps, out of breath and gasping, "Wow!"

Customers purchase emotions with their money. When life gets too stressful, they call a travel agent and book a cruise or a vacation. Or they buy a motorcycle and speed down back roads with the wind whistling by their ears. Or they purchase a new fishing rod and drive up to the lake for a weekend. They part with their hard-earned money for the fun, the relaxation, and the excitement, not the trip, the bike, or the rod and reel. When a person is sore, he or she books a massage expecting to luxuriate in the oils, lotions, soothing music and pain relief. After the neighbor's house gets robbed, they buy a security system and pay someone to install it. But they aren't buying the sensors or cameras; they are purchasing the feeling of safety. Similarly, they acquire insurance not for the policy, but for the peace of mind, the freedom not to worry. *Good salespeople sell feelings.* They sell fun whenever they have the opportunity.

I've studied humor for years. In fact, almost 20 years ago, I wrote a book called *The Twelve Immutable Laws of Humor* describing the dozen factors that make a person funny. Humor is a tricky business because politically correct hypersensitivity has amplified the risk that hearers might become instantly offended. However, if you can discipline yourself to use only jokes that are firmly ensconced in the ever-narrowing safe zone, using humor can increase your sales. A decade ago MBA students at Rutgers University, Lehigh University, and DePaul University conducted a study in which contract negotiations were begun by first sending the customer a Dilbert cartoon, one that had been carefully screened and adjudged to be both funny and inoffensive. Results were compared against a control group who conducted their negotiations as normal (that is, without the cartoon). Just the simple gesture of lightening the mood at the beginning of the sales negotiation process increased sales by 15%. The level of satisfaction on both sides also increased, and participants tended to start the process by offering more reasonable terms for the transaction.

I once heard a waiter brag that he always told his customers a funny joke just before leaving the check on the table, and he received more in tips than all of the other wait staff. Jenna McNight, a blogger who is also a customer of Zappos (an online shoe retailer), recorded the following interaction with the company:

> *Zappos: We've successfully received your Zappos.com order, and our elves are working double-time to get it ready to ship. Did you know that elves work at twice the speed of humans and only require sugar for nourishment? It's a fact.*

> *Jenna McNight: I will be sure to put sugar in my payment envelope. I hope your Receiving Department shares it with fellow workers.*

> *Zappos: I'm sure they will share, after all, elves are excellent sharers.*

The lesson to be learned is that injecting humor into your business transactions improves trust, increases sales, and relieves tension.

It should be noted that humor is not a substitute for great customer service. An employee's jokes and antics might actually be off-putting when service is bad, as customers may assume that they are interacting with a clown who doesn't take his or her job seriously. Humor, for this reason, must be well-timed and used to elevate great service to an even higher level, not to excuse or make light of mistakes. Moreover, in some cultures humor is deemed inappropriate in the workplace and might actually harm the negotiation process, so be sure to do your homework before taking your vaudeville act/sales presentation overseas. The other danger is that the same *shtick* repeated over and over becomes stale and loses its effectiveness with time. The first few times I heard a Southwest Airlines flight attendant turn the preflight safety talk into a series of humorous one-liners, I found it entertaining. However, after twenty-plus years the same old jokes have worn thin. While I'm sure they leave a positive impression on those who fly only rarely, I suspect that those who fly Southwest Airlines all the time find it annoying. Since I'm a loyal United customer, I find myself on a Southwest Airlines flight only 2 or 3 times per year, and I make it a point to put on my headphones and listen to an audio book during the "performance." I'm of the opinion that the airline should ban certain jokes that have been used so often that they are predictable and routine. The one-liners should be refreshed regularly. I did, however, hear a new one recently. As I boarded a three-fourths empty SWA flight the attendant remarked. "We request that all passengers take a widow seat and press your faces firmly to the glass so that our competition will think we're full." The entire plane burst out laughing!

Make people laugh, and you raise their estimation of your company accordingly.

Exercise Questions:

1. What can you do to make buying your product or service more fun?

2. Are there any topics that should be avoided in your attempts at humor?

3. Can the décor of your website or workplace or your wardrobe be spruced up to seem more playful?

4. What ways can you think of that would make your emails more fun to read?

Chapter 11

DAZZLE THEM WITH ATMOSPHERE

While it is of little importance to me, my wife is keenly aware of the atmosphere of any given business establishment and it plays a significant role in determining whether she will ever darken their doors. There is a Mexican restaurant near our home that is quite convenient and the service is acceptable, though not dazzling. The place is well decorated, the food is somewhere between good and great, and the prices are very attractive. But my wife gets a disgusted look on her face whenever I suggest going there. She recoils and her eyes become mere slits as she shakes her head in tiny side-to-side motions as though she's having *delirium tremens*. She protests, "It's too loud in there!" Hers is not a carefully thought-out analysis of the pros and cons of dining in that location; it is an instantaneous and visceral reaction of revulsion to the place. In my opinion, her dislike of the restaurant is unfortunate. I like it, and I drive past it several times every week. Instead, we eat at a more laid-back place (in a direction I rarely travel) where the food is no better. The prices there are about the same and the dining room is not as well-decorated, but it is *quiet*. In my view, the loud place is loud because so many people love it enough to eat there even though they must shout across their tables to one another loudly enough to be heard over the din. I'm happy to pay the price of talking loudly in order to enjoy the restaurant's terrific qualities. To my wife, though, the loud atmosphere is a deal killer.

My wife sometimes has a similarly horrified reaction when I suggest she run down to a nearby retail store to pick up some needed items, moaning, "It's too junky!" She instead drives three minutes further to pay higher prices at a store that boasts neat and wide aisles. In my opinion, it's quite impressive that the junkier store manages to stock a variety of items almost rivaling Walmart in less than one-tenth of the floor space, but I often get overruled. The atmosphere of the messy store depresses her and she reacts visibly. On the rare occasions I can coax her to shop there in order to take advantage of the bargain prices, she behaves as though all of the other shoppers are lepers, the floor covered with snakes, and every shelf infested with smallpox virus. She slinks through the store, elbows together to make herself as skinny as possible so as not to brush against the supposedly-tainted items that dangle from every shelf and to avoid the boxes of items that clutter the aisles. In some places, there's not even room for two shoppers to pass one another without turning sideways and brushing against one another. The other store (the one with big, wide aisles), on the other hand, elevates her spirits. She feels that she can stroll casually through the store and luxuriate in the wide open spaces rather than tiptoeing and zigzagging. She lets the spaciousness fill her soul like a breath of fresh air. A trip down the coffee aisle soothes the olfactory sense with the aroma freshly ground beans. The slightly higher prices are, to her, a small price to pay for the more pleasant sights and smells that make her feel so free.

The great challenge of providing an uplifting and pleasant atmosphere is that when human beings repeatedly experience a negative stimulus over an extended period of time, they tend to stop noticing it. Like the smell that enveloped my elderly aunt's house when I was a boy and made visitors gag, she and her husband were inured to it because they had become "nose blind." The odor had probably developed incrementally over a period of many years and they slowly adjusted to it. About 20 years ago I got married and my wife and I combined all our belongings and moved them into our new house. Once all the furniture, paintings and knickknacks had been distributed among the rooms, we couldn't help but notice that the walls in the living room remained barren. They were almost blinding in their whiteness, so we vowed to quickly buy some type of décor to break up the garish monotony. Several months later, however, I was watching a football game on television in that same room and suddenly realized that the walls were still bare. We had simply stopped noticing. But I suspect that every guest we had in our home thinks we're clueless decorators! (Full disclosure, I actually *am*, but my wife isn't.)

I used to do consulting with churches who wanted to know how they might grow their attendance and membership. In our phone call previous to my visit there, the pastor of one medium-sized church assured me that his facility was warm and inviting. But within a few minutes of my arrival at the church I was shocked by what I saw. A dirty mop bucket sat in the corner of the quite small men's room filled with smelly and dirty water. The bulletin board in the lobby was cluttered with scores of unrelated, disorganized pieces of paper advertising events that had long since come and gone. A stack of hymnals with sheet music dangling from them stood in the corner of the sanctuary. When I pointed these items out, the baffled minister replied, "They've all been like that for so long we've stopped noticing." One thing is certain, however. Visitors noticed them and were discouraged by those factors from returning.

One of the most important aspects of any brick-and-mortar business is the cleanliness (or filthiness) of its restrooms. Few aspects of a building become so instantly and deeply tattooed onto the memory as the appearance of the lavatories. One disgusting experience may be enough to keep any given customer from ever returning. On the other hand, people might make a beeline for an establishment with consistently clean restrooms. In Texas, a convenience store chain called Buc-ee's burst onto the scene in 2001 by opening a massive roadside store boasting about 100 gas pumps (not a misprint), a bakery, a deli, and a huge selection of candies, drinks, and snacks. Their "convenience stores" are bigger than some Walmarts, and on any given day one can see stunned tourists taking panoramic photos or videos of the interior to show their friends. But their chief claim to fame is that their bathrooms look as though they belong in a Ritz Carlton. They are *huge* (featuring more than 80 toilets) and pristine, and maintained 24 hours a day. They even won a national contest hosted by the Cintas Corporation for the cleanest restrooms in America. The very idea that a convenience store bathroom could rank ahead of every luxury department store, hotel and restaurant in the country is astounding, and this laurel no doubt puts them at the top of the list of places to stop along the highway when you just have to go.

For brick-and-mortar establishments in which customers physically enter your store or office, playing the right kind of music can add just the right touch to your atmosphere, just as the wrong kind of music can detract from it. Many malls play pleasant music in the background that has been proven to positively influence how long customers linger in stores and, more importantly, how much they spend. If you're selling racing boats or motocross bikes you'll want adrenaline-pumping music that makes the heart race to add to the thrill-seeker's motivation. Getting a massage to the same music would be counterproductive. Slow tempo music has been demonstrated to improve sales in most locales, but you must be careful not to lull your customers to sleep. You want them to stay in the store, not drive home to take a nap! Those who master the concept of The Magic Touch realize that your product is not merely goods and services, but a comprehensive experience.

Riggs' Law of Customer Serivce

Perhaps surprisingly, there is often a direct correlation between how managers treat employees and how the employees, in turn, treat customers. Every business or organization possesses external employees and internal ones. The external customer is the shopper, the diner, the policyholder, etc. These are the people referred to when the word customer is used unmodified. Internal customers are one's fellow employees. I would like to share with you what I call "Riggs' Law of Customer Service:" External service eventually rises or falls to the level of internal service. Stated another way, the manner in which employees treat each other (and, in particular, the manner in which supervisors treat their direct reports) will eventually be reflected in the way that staff members treat external customers. It is impossible to improve the customer experience for very long without first tending to the employee experience.

Riggs' Law works almost as unfailingly as the law of gravity because all human beings are subject to the influence of passive-aggressive behavior, which reliably predicts that when people are treated badly they will retaliate, sometimes in subtle ways. While people offended outside the sphere of their workplaces might react loudly and aggressively, most employees will choose the safer route: invisible or indirect methods to strike back. They will not openly try to harm their bosses (which would be suicidal for their careers), but they will become less helpful than they otherwise would have been, which is potentially just as bad, for it occurs invisibly. For example, if the boss yells at a cashier, she'll probably be too smart to scream back. The consequences would be too severe. Instead, she'll just be rude to the next customer she encounters, who might then never come back. This reaction will harm the boss just as much, but in a fashion that cannot be easily traced back to its perpetrator. If you call your executive assistant an idiot, he won't respond by calling you a moron. He values his job. Rather than attacking you personally, he'll just choose to be less helpful in achieving company goals. He'll stop coming in early or staying late the way he once did. He'll lengthen his lunch hour by 10 minutes each day and not work as hard as he used to. The quality of his work will decline. On the other hand, if he is treated really well, he will likely come to work with enthusiasm and increase his productivity.

I and a friend joined forces a few years to do all of the customer service training for the San Francisco Department of Health. After one of my training sessions, a nurse wrote the following on her comment card:

> *"I feel my manager is a hypocrite. They ignore me and treat me like a second class citizen and then wonder why I don't provide great service to the patients. Until you can begin to treat me with a little respect, don't expect me to give good service."*

If a nurse will give less than her best effort to create a restorative, pleasant and positive atmosphere when the health or even the life of of her customer might be on the line, doesn't it make sense to believe that your employees will do less than their best when the only thing at stake is whether you get a raise, bonus, or promotion? One of the most important things you can do to improve the atmosphere in your organization is to be kind to your people. When staff members feel they have been treated well, it becomes the natural response of the human heart for most people (sadly, not all) to want to give their absolute best.

Exercise Questions:

1. What does your place of business look like?

2. Does it have (or could it have) any aromas that would please customers?

3. Is it too loud or harried? Or not enough?

4. Does the vibe of your business match your products or your company culture?

5. Would background music improve the atmosphere? If so, what style of music?

6. Do employees feel that they are treated so well that they want to help build the company up?

Chapter 12

DAZZLE THEM WITH USER-FRIENDLINESS

When a customer anticipates doing business with you, how does that make them feel? Do they envision themselves having a simple, easy interaction with you? Or do they visualize themselves enduring a torturous experience that will make them want to shoot themselves before it's all over? Do they dread doing business with you? Or are they confident that their transaction will be as simple as 1-2-3? Staples office supply stores advertise that shopping with them is as simple as pushing an "easy button." Whether they live up to this slogan or not is an open question. However, the fact that the ease of doing business with a given establishment forms a factor in determining their buying patterns is not. Customers will delay calling or visiting your business, or avoid it all together if they have reason to believe the buying process will be complicated or painful.

The Worst Airline in the Skies

When I first became an itinerant motivational speaker in the mid-90s the worst airline in the skies, by far, was Continental (The airline has since merged with United). Out of about 10 major national airlines they ranked dead last in customer satisfaction in almost every single category. They were worst in baggage handling, on-time performance, customer complaints, and more. Their only positive rating was in safety which, to be fair, must be conceded as the most important of them all.

Continental rarely flew on time, *and they didn't care.* I avoided them whenever possible. However, on those rare occasions when my schedule required me to book a flight on Continental, I went into a 30-minute depression in anticipation of the distress and agony they were almost certain to inflict on me. I dreaded going to the airport on those days. The airline was hemorrhaging money due to having to constantly transfer tickets from their existing (few) passengers to other airlines due to delays and cancellations. I had no way of knowing that this was all about to change, and almost overnight.

In 1995, Continental's CEO, Gordon Bethune, hired a 34-year-old named Greg Brenneman as their Chief Operating Officer. Why hire one so young to lead a billion-dollar business? Apparently, no one else would take the job, lest any association with Continental Airlines might appear as a blight on the resume of anyone who already possessed a positive reputation as a manager. But together, Bethune and Brenneman turned the airline around almost instantaneously, rocketing from the bottom of the pile to the top in only 6 months. His secret? He turned over control of customer interactions to the individual employees.

When Brenneman arrived at Continental, the company culture was one of rules and prohibitions. Whenever a flight attendant, gate agent, or ticket agent made a concession or gesture in an attempt to keep a passenger happy or pacify an angry one, the lawyers and bankers who ran the company would immediately fire off a memo strictly forbidding that particular action. The missives were compiled in a notebook sarcastically known among airline employees as the "Thou Shalt Not Book." By 1995, Brenneman claims the notebook was 9 inches thick (not a typo)! Employees were, in effect, hogtied. Since no one could possibly know, let alone remember and instantly recall, which actions were verboten and which were allowed, no one dared run the risk of getting in trouble. In order to avoid being reprimanded, employees simply took the safe route and said, "No" to almost any and every request. Happy passengers who could have remained so instead became dissatisfied, then disgruntled. Frustrated customers became angry. Angry ones just left. Continental was simply too hard to do business with.

Brenneman held a ceremony with employees shortly after he arrived. He threw the "Thou Shalt Not Book" in a barrel in a parking lot, covered it with lighter fluid, and set it afire. The new policy became, "Let the inmates run the asylum." The innovative culture became one of, "Do whatever you think is in the best interest of the airline and our passengers." There were guidelines, of course. Employees couldn't enter into contracts to buy 737s from Boeing. But they were freed to be kind and responsive. Suddenly, the airline became user-friendly. I now know that when I do business with United Airlines, I'll be treated well and that the process will usually be quite smooth. I also deal with car rental companies all the time, and they serve as a wonderful example of this principle, too.

There are a couple of rental agencies that I try to avoid, simply because they are so difficult to work with. Those outfits make me stand in line for 15 minutes, then watch idly as they type information into their computers for another 5 minutes, make me sign or initial a long contract in 5 to 8 places, then allow me to go find my car. Sometimes they go out into the lot and walk with me around the car taking note of existing scratches or dents. Avis and Hertz, however, are different. They often text me an hour or two before my reservation time to tell me where to find my car. I walk there, start the car, and drive off, just stopping for one minute at the exit to show my I.D. Don't assume that this is just because I have been renting from these two companies for years. The same is true of the companies that I avoid, yet those agencies *still* force me to jump through all the same hoops as those with no credit and no history of past patronage. I've rented from those less-trusting businesses from time to time for thirty years and never failed to return the car on time and in perfect condition, but still they don't trust me enough to hand me the keys. User-friendliness is a *culture*, and it sometimes makes all the difference. User-friendliness also applies after the sale as well as before. That's why your refund policy is critical.

I mentioned earlier that I shop regularly at The Home Depot. I love their variety and prices. But best of all, I feel completely safe shopping there. Why? Because they instantly refund my money for any product I purchased there. It's a no-risk proposition for me because they assume all of the liability in almost every transaction. Sometimes I'll discover an unused item in my garage that I purchased a year or two earlier and never opened. No problem! I just take it back to The Home Depot, they scan the item and give me store credit for the amount of the purchase. They would give the money back to me in cash if I still had the receipt, but since I shop there every week store credit is just as good. They even have a separate cash register lane just for returns and there's rarely more than one person ahead of me when I go there to get a refund. The return is smooth, guiltless, friendly, and easy.

One of the fastest ways to make your customer say, "Wow" is to offer to refund their money *on the spot*, no questions asked. Of course, if you're selling very expensive items that can't be put back in inventory and resold, like newly installed kitchen cabinets, you may not be able to do this. But if you're selling mops or jewelry or plane tickets, there's nothing that disarms and wins over a disgruntled customer faster than a cheerful and immediate offer of a refund or exchange. This policy puts teeth in the saying, "Satisfaction guaranteed."

Walmart founder Sam Walton built his empire on the assumption that 97% of customers are hard-working, honest people who would never return an item if they felt they had gotten their money's worth. Even if an item had been purchased two or three years earlier, he instructed his employees to refund people's money on the spot, no questions asked. When a customer knows that he will *always* get his money back if dissatisfied, he comes back to that establishment over and over again with full confidence that he'll never be stuck with an item that doesn't live up to his expectations.

Of course, there are unethical people that will abuse this policy. Walton related the story of a man who bought a set of golf clubs from Walmart, then returned a few days later to return them because one of them was badly bent. The man had obviously hit a tree with the club, but claimed it had been that way when he opened the box. True to his policy, Walton immediately exchanged the clubs for a brand new set. Some would conclude that Walmart lost lots of money on the exchange. A more long-term view, however, is that the dishonest man probably continued to shop at Walmart for many years to come, more than making up for the cost of one set of golf clubs. Moreover, Walton reportedly kept the bent club in his office as a memento and displayed it for many years to graphically demonstrate to his employees how lenient their refund policy actually was. On another occasion, he accepted a return of a Craftsman tool, a brand that is only sold at Sears. Why? He told the customer he would take the item back because he wanted that patron to come to Walmart the next time he needed a tool.

The speed of the refund is critical, too. The refund must be immediate, cheerful and unequivocal. No sneers of suspicion, no rolled eyes, no expressions of distrust, no hesitation. The policy must be clear to every employee who deals with customers so that they do not need to call a manager to approve the return. User-friendliness should also dictate the layout of your online presence.

Websites must be easy to use. Your logo should be prominently plastered in the upper left-hand corner of your site (the first place the eye naturally goes) so that visitors instantly know they've found the right business. Contact information should be easy to find, along with social media icons. The website must be secure to avoid scaring off purchasers. Functionality should be smooth and all links must work. Every "landing page" (that is, any page on your site that a web search might possibly lead to first) should have links back to your home page or to other similar goods or services you offer for sale. Bullet points make it simpler for visitors to find the information they're looking for. Above all, they must be fully responsive so that those searching on their phones will see the entire site, not having to move the image about to read a headline or see an entire graphic.

Exercise Questions:

1. How can you make your company easier to do business with?

2. When you do business with people, who assumes the risk?

3. Should you reform your return policy?

4. Should you retrain your employees with this in mind?

SECTION TWO

THE
MAGIC TOUCH

Chapter 13

THE GREATEST SHOW ON EARTH

The best-known magician of all time was the great Harry Houdini. His genius was not merely that of a conjurer or escape artist, but a marketer. He was the quintessential showman. He publicly challenged law enforcement in the capitals of Europe to see if they could keep him locked up (they never did). He quite publicly sued a German police officer who claimed that the great magician was a fraud who had achieved his escapes by bribing captors. He won the suit. On one occasion in Moscow, the master showman escaped from a Siberian prison transport van, claiming that had he failed he would have had to travel all the way to Siberia. While this is highly doubtful, the newspapers all ran the story as though it were true, further enhancing his legend. He immigrated to the United States and hung upside down from a skyscraper while escaping from a straitjacket. He then had himself shackled and restrained, placed in a locked trunk and tossed into a river, managing to escape before drowning. In every case, he made certain that the press was there to cover the riveting spectacle. He mastered the art of getting the news media to provide free advertising for him. When copycats began to duplicate his handcuff routine, he abandoned it and challenged the citizenry to devise their own scenarios and devices that would test his skills as an escape artist. He freed himself from milk cans filled with water, from trunks nailed and riveted shut, even from the stomach of a whale that had washed up on Boston's shore. However, he left one challenge incomplete, an endurance stunt never performed due to his sudden and unexpected death on October 31, 1926. Even in death, bizarrely, he augmented his legendary status by appropriately succumbing on Halloween.

Magician David Blaine was, like so many aspiring artists, a talented nobody. He made his living doing magic tricks on the streets of New York City for tips, striving tenaciously to get in front of celebrities whose images might be used alongside his to gain notoriety. His genius was not that he was a fantastic magician (he's quite good, but no better than hundreds of others), but that he created a new way of exhibiting his illusions to the public. The focus of the camera was not so much on the amazing *effects* he performed, but on the amazing *affect* it had on those watching. The star of the show wasn't the mild-mannered, low-key Blaine, but on the audience members freaking out in response to them. Though magic has existed as an entertainment form for centuries, no one had ever filmed it from this perspective. The added bonus, of course, was that any trick could be performed and filmed dozens of times, each with a different audience, and only the most extreme reaction would be included in the final version aired on television. The impression created was that his every trick left audiences shrieking in astonishment. This technique gained name recognition for Blaine, but stardom would have to wait until he found a way to focus the eyes of the world on him, not the audience.

In 1999, Blaine chose to perform the stunt Houdini never had the opportunity to attempt. On April 5, 1999, Blaine had himself entombed below ground in a transparent casket outside Trump Place in Manhattan, with a three-ton clear water tank above him to prevent his escape that nevertheless allowed passersby to view him through it. The box was barely big enough to house his body and left virtually no room for movement. He reportedly survived on only three tablespoons of water per day, and his only communication with the "surface" was a hand buzzer that could be activated in case of emergency. A week later, as the tank was pumped dry and his casket lifted from the hole, hundreds of news outlets were present to ensure that his name would be heard by hundreds of millions of people that day. He had mastered Houdini's secret: If you can wow the press, *they will then wow your customers for you*. It's almost like magic, but you don't have to be a magician to pull it off.

Near my home in Austin, Texas is a sporting goods store called Cabela's. It specializes in hunting, fishing and camping gear, none of which interest me much. Now that I've retired as the Scoutmaster of my son's Boy Scout troop, my camping days are behind me. In fact, I only ventured into tent-living for those scouting years because I believe in the movement and care about the boys. But I never enjoyed the living outdoors part. Likewise, I get bored playing golf, so you can imagine my level of ennui should I venture out to drop a line in a creek and sit silently for hours in hopes of a nibble on my trout line! And I've not been hunting since I was 12. Nevertheless, I love to go to Cabela's! It's not just a store, it's a tourist destination. At the center-rear of the store is an artificial mountain dotted with scores of stuffed and mounted exotic animals from all over the world. And, of course, when I go there to marvel at the attraction, I wind up spending money on a new windbreaker, a thermos, or a hotdog from their café. If they hadn't sought to be an attraction, however, I would never darken their doors. I wouldn't venture into an outdoorsman's store for the products. I would never be a *satisfied* customer because I would never visit the establishment at all.

The new paradigm advocated in this book is that great customer service is not merely a series of conscientious or impressive behaviors and pleasant customer interactions; it is rather a *show*. Customer service has given way to a customer *experience*. Employees view themselves not as cashiers, receptionists, or shelf-stockers, but as actors in a grand play. They are thespians playing the roles of the world's greatest customer service providers. They do not just arrive at work; they answer their cues to appear onstage in character and begin their act. This is how you transform a customer interaction into a customer experience. This is how you turn service that pleases into a circus that enthralls.

Companies that manage to transform merely good service into a live, never-ending improv act thereby set themselves apart from their competitors by creating an almost magical experience. Staff members ask themselves moment by moment, "What would the best employee in the world do?" Service transforms not merely into an activity, *but a spectacle*. Workers are not merely staff members, but *cast* members. (In fact, all Disney parks call their employees "cast members" to reinforce this understanding.) The opening of the front door each morning is akin to the rising of a stage curtain rather than merely turning a key to signal the beginning of eight more hours of drudgery. Each employee is onstage and in character for *every second* that they are in view (or within earshot) of their audience, the customer. They know their roles and goals, though the script is being written spontaneously throughout the performance.

The only type of service that engenders customer loyalty is the type that wows, creating a moment of pure magic that shimmers in the memory and injects a powerful shot of endorphins the way your first kiss did. It stands out in the mind because it was so completely unexpected, above and beyond the norm, so *different*. That is what this book is about. You don't want customer service; you want a customer circus. You seek smiles and amazement. You strive to grab your customer's attention the way a high-wire act or lion taming act does. Your aim is to raise hairs on the back of your customer's necks and drop their jaws in response to the pleasantly unexpected. Your goal must be to entertain with the flare of P.T. Barnum, the fun of clowns and balloons, the rehearsed precision of a flying trapeze act, and the novelty of dancing bears. You want your customer walking away thinking, "Wow! I've never experienced anything like that in my life!" Your wish is that they call their friends and relatives afterward to tell them, "You have got to go see this for yourself!"

P. T. Barnum in 1865 wrote his classic book, *Humbugs of the World*, describing his secrets for success. He specialized in displaying curiosities and was always in search of a larger-than-life exhibit that would create headlines and draw crowds. The word humbug, as he defined it, "consists in putting on glittering appearances…, novel expedients, by which to suddenly arrest public attention, and attract the public eye and ear." Human curiosities (people who were extremely old, small, overweight, etc.) were a popular form of entertainment in that era and this fascination formed the star to which Barnum hitched his wagon. In our day, of course, such displays are considered unseemly at best and unacceptably cruel or criminal at worst. Yet, the principle remains true that in order to dazzle your customers you must find something that will galvanize their attention and make them eager to experience your offerings for themselves.

I am a huge fan of a little-remembered Chicago architect by the name of Daniel Hudson Burnham. On a trip to the area a few years ago I even set aside a half-day to see if I could find his grave so that I could pay my respects. I located it on a tiny island in a small pond tucked away at the extreme back corner of Chicago's massive Graceland Cemetery. The small, nondescript tombstone he shares with his wife makes no mention of the man's signature achievement. Daniel Burnham was the creative genius and driving force behind the Chicago World's Fair of 1893. The fair's official name was the Columbian Exposition, in honor of the 400th anniversary of Columbus' landing in the new world (even though late by a year). He was tasked on a mere three years' notice to conceive, design, construct, and open the gates on a World's Fair so grand that it would eclipse even the Paris World's Fair that in 1889 had featured the unveiling of the Eiffel

Tower as her main entrance. He succeeded in grand, jaw-dropping style. The world had never seen anything like the Chicago World's Fair, and the world has never seen anything like it since.

In under 36 months, Daniel Burnham, assisted by world-famous landscape architect Frank Law Olmstead, transformed a worthless 700-acre swamp on Chicago's southeast side bordering Lake Michigan into the glittering White City of canals, colonnades, sculptures, fountains, and buildings of indescribable scale. In those scant three years he oversaw the construction of 238 buildings, five of which were among the 7 largest ever constructed up until that time. Only Versailles (outside Paris) and The Winter Palace in St. Petersburg, Russia could compare for sheer size.

The sight was so astounding that first time viewers were said to gasp in amazement, stand dumbstruck in awe, or even burst into tears are the sheer glory of the place. A young man named Frank Baum was so taken with the spectacle that years later, as he penned *The Wizard of Oz*, he painted the place green in his imagination and dubbed it "Emerald City."

The Manufacturers and Liberal Arts Build-ing (pictured on the right, crowned with flags), at a million square feet, was the largest building ever constructed up until that time, and would not be eclipsed until the opening of the Pentagon five decades later. The largest pyramid in Egypt could fit inside without touching a wall or the ceiling. Before the fair officially opened, a hundred thousand peo-ple attended a concert *in just one end of it*. The building eventually housed 3 million exhibits and could accommodate tens of thousands of fairgoers as they wandered its many aisles. Yet, this mammoth structure comprised only a tiny fraction of the fair. At 700 acres, the Columbian Exposition was more than six times the size of Disney's Magic Kingdom (including parking lots!) in Orlando, Florida. And every acre would be needed.

The crowds drawn by the fair were enormous. On Saturday, October 9, 1893, more than 750,000 people purchased admission to the fair. To put that number in perspective, that number represents more than 7 times the highest single-day attendance in the history of Disney's Magic Kingdom. Fully one percent of the entire nation's population attended the fair on that day! This number becomes even more astounding when you consider that every single one of those three-quarters of a million people arrived by foot, horse, or train, for there were no cars or planes in that era.

Burnham envisioned almost everything in the fair as bigger, bolder, and newer than anything anyone had ever conceived. The fair featured the world's first indoor ice skating rink and the world's first use of alternating current. Most people in that day had only seen a few electric lights in their entire lives, but were greeted by 120,000 of them after sunset each evening. It created the brightest nightscape in history and consumed more electricity than the entire city of Chicago. To top the Eiffel Tower, the fair featured the world's first Ferris Wheel, which stood 264 feet tall and boasted cars that could hold up to 72 passengers each. When full, it carried a staggering 2100 people (roughly double the capacity of today's largest Ferris Wheel, the High Roller in Las Vegas, Nevada). The giant wheel was placed in the center of a strip of land called the Midway Plaissance (still the name of the street that bisects it today), and for this reason the part of any fair that contains carnival rides is, to this day, called the "midway." Sadly, the entire fair burned to the ground a few months after the exposition closed, and the area is now covered with soccer fields, parking lots, a marina, and marsh. My favorite quote from Daniel Burnham is this:

Make no little plans; they have no magic to stir men's blood and probably themselves will not be realized. Make big plans; aim high in hope and work, remembering that a noble, logical diagram once recorded will never die, but long after we are gone be a living thing, asserting itself with ever-growing insistency.

The message, even though penned in archaic language, is clear: think big. Strive to capture people's attention and make them say, "Wow!" Don't just open a business. Put on a show!

When you attend a live play or show, one thing is certain: the actors will not be caught off-guard chit-chatting with one another when the curtain rises (or if they do, they won't be employed for very long!). They will not pull out their smartphones to surf the web onstage if they get bored with the dialogue. They will not leave stage unless the script calls for them to exit. They will not be caught slouching or smoking unless their character was created as a sloucher or a smoker. They will not step out of character for a moment unless the plot requires that they leave the stage and until they are completely out of sight. Even then, they will not talk loudly while backstage if there is any possibility of being heard by the audience, remaining cognizant at all times that a live performance is underway, and that the reviews are certain to produce a buzz—for good or bad.

I have on a few occasions attended plays put on by amateurs at a local theater. Because the actors are not professionals, it is not uncommon to see an actor leave stage—though still visible in the wings to some members of the audience—and immediately drop their shoulders, change their pace and abandon their character. They fold their arms and watch from the wings, perhaps whispering in the ear of another off-stage colleague, not caring that people on the front few rows along the walls can still see them. A true professional never leaves character until he or she is completely out of view from every audience member, every customer. But just because your customer service is planned doesn't mean that it has to be canned.

Leonardo DiCaprio, while filming *Django Unchained*, slammed his fist on a glass table so hard that it unexpectedly shattered, slicing his hand in the process. Undaunted, DiCaprio continued in his role even as blood dripped from his fingers. This take made it into the final cut of the film. While portraying Abraham Lincoln in the film *Lincoln*, Daniel Day Lewis, a Brit, refused to speak in his normal voice—even off camera—for the duration of the shoot, choosing instead to remain in character as the iconic president even while talking on the phone to friends. Before the late Heath Ledger played Batman's nemesis, The Joker, in *The Dark Knight*, he locked himself in his apartment for a month in an attempt to drive himself to the point of madness so that he could understand his demented character. During the shoot, he refused to respond to any question directed at Heath Ledger, the actor, but would instead respond as he imagined The Joker would have done. This obsessive and excessive practice may have contributed to his untimely death before the film was released. The lesson they teach is not that employees should greet their friends after work by saying, "Welcome to Acme! How can I help you?" but that they should remain in character for every second that they are on the job, and spend their down time imagining how they might improve the act.

When I'm in Denver, Colorado I love to eat at Casa Bonita, a Mexican food buffet oddly tucked away in a nondescript strip mall east of downtown. The food is not particularly good, in my opinion, but it is plentiful. The service is average. But the décor is quite fancy and evokes images of a Cinco de Mayo celebration in Mexico City. Waiters and waitresses are adorned in colorful traditional Mexican costumes. But Casa Bonita sets itself apart from all other restaurants by scheduling shows that can be viewed from many of the dining tables. Cliff divers emerge every couple of hours to leap from a 30 foot platform into a deep pool. The amazing demonstration alternates with swordfights, puppet shows, and gunfights, holding children and adults alike spellbound. The human psyche is attracted to pleasure and novelty, and companies that manage to trigger these two impulses naturally rise to the top. When customer service is elevated to the level of a performance, patrons don't just wander in when they need an item; they make a beeline for your business whenever they can.

Unlike the theater, business reviews aren't written up and published by professional critics in the entertainment sections of newspapers. Rather, they are published on Facebook, tweeted on Twitter, recorded on Yelp!, even video-recorded and documented on YouTube. Unlike the reviews printed in newspapers of old, those published on the internet never go away, and are retrievable by anyone in the world in milliseconds! These negative reviews can be brutal, resulting in long-lasting devastation. That's why providing The Magic Touch is so vital.

Exercise Questions:

1. How can you train employees to see themselves as actors in a play rather than merely helpers?

2. Describe how behaviors would change if employees viewed themselves as improv actors who are onstage.

3. Should employees' wardrobes be changed to help transform service into a show?

4. Is there anything new, different, or novel that can be included in your business or customer service that would cause your company to become a destination?

Chapter 14

The Critics Get Their Day

In a recent training event I conducted I asked members of the audience to share customer service horror stories they had experienced in the past. Those in attendance came from many different professions, including hairdressers, restaurant employees, bank tellers and about ten employees of a local company that builds swimming pools. When it was her turn, a middle-aged woman pointed at the pool company manager and emphatically said, "I had a horrible experience with *them*!" The manager looked stunned and turned ashen. Sensing a teachable moment, I encouraged her to tell us her story.

She told of how she had found the company in the phone book Yellow Pages and called them for a quote. She informed the man who answered the phone that she was thinking about building a pool in her backyard. The man asked, "What is your budget for the pool?"

She replied, "About twenty-four thousand dollars."

He responded, "We don't build pools that cheaply." The conversation then ended, leaving the woman feeling insulted and angry. In her mind, he had all but called her a cheapskate or trailer trash! As she recounted the conversation to my audience that day, she became so angry that she visibly trembled with rage. In order to drive home the point I was trying to make to my trainees, I asked her, "How many people have you told this story to?"

She replied: "Hundreds. Everybody I know."

The manager of the pool company had by now turned completely pale.

I then asked the woman, "When did this happen?"

Her reply shocked everyone in the room. "1996," she said.

After nearly two decades that single abrupt phone conversation still infuriated her to the degree that she felt compelled to do everything in her power to dissuade her friends, family and acquaintances from hiring that particular pool company. Given the price of a typical pool in Texas, she had quite possibly cost that company hundreds of thousands of dollars in revenue. The sad fact was that every single solitary employee of that company (including ownership and management) had turned over during that time. Yet they were still paying dearly for one bad review garnered by a cast member that had long since left the show, and had only been "onstage" with this customer for a few seconds.

To make matters worse, gone are the days when the only damage this woman could inflict was by speaking to the few people she knew who just happened to be ready to install a pool in their backyards. Her negative word-of-mouth advertising would certainly be somewhat contained as those who heard her story would soon forget the conversation, or at least which pool company had insulted her. The effects of her words would in this way be mitigated over time. In the 21st century, however, there is almost no way to contain the blaze. The fire of her fury would burn in internet eternity in full view of anyone seeking to build a pool. She would not have to ever cross paths with prospective pool buyers, for they would proactively seek out her review and find it online in mere milliseconds. Locating a review for a pool company used to be akin to finding a needle in a haystack. Now, the internet serves as a gigantic magnet that instantaneously pulls out every needle from a thousand haystacks. Worse still, the internet never forgets. The name of that pool company, had the offending action occurred a mere decade later, would be forever enshrined beside her caustic evaluation. The best that company could hope for would be to overwhelm her criticism with scores of positive reviews, or to issue an online rebuttal or apology to dilute its venom. This fire might never be extinguished. It must be beaten back and defeated every day forever. It will smolder for years and at any second might silently scorch the company once more from the anonymity of cyberspace.

I and my family moved from Austin, Texas almost 4 years ago to a small bedroom community 20 miles west. Shortly thereafter I chipped a front tooth and decided this was a good opportunity to begin the search for a dentist close to our new home. Less than two miles from my driveway there sat an old house which a dentist had converted into his office. I walked in unannounced and found the counter unmanned, but shortly thereafter a nice woman presented herself in a white smock, obviously doing double duty as the hygienist and intake clerk. I explained my situation and she checked me in to await an appointment with the dentist. I provided her with my insurance card, but mistakenly gave her my Humana *health* insurance card instead of my Humana dental insurance card (they look identical when I'm not wearing reading glasses). She photocopied it and before long I was in the dentist's chair. He was competent and knowledgeable, but a bit of a curmudgeon. I immediately determined that while I would be quite open to making this man my regular dentist, my wife would feel quite differently. I silently decided that I would not return, even though I was satisfied with my experience. The chip in my tooth was a minor one, so the dentist merely filed the rough edges off the tooth and sent me on my way. That's when things got interesting.

A week or two later, I received a bill in the mail for several hundred dollars for the procedure and a notice that my insurance company had declined payment for the dental procedure. (*Of course it did.* I had provided them with the wrong insurance card.) I suddenly realized my mistake and called them expecting to read them the correct policy number over the phone so they could resend all the paperwork to Humana. All they had to do was scratch out the wrong number, write in the correct one, and re-fax the already filled-out forms. Instead, the hygienist informed me that they are "not required" to refile for insurance, and that I should write them a check for the full amount, then file a claim with Humana Dental directly. When I inquired where I might find the correct forms, she replied that she would mail me the paperwork to fill out and submit to the company. Stunningly, she did not send me the *completed* paperwork, but instead mailed me the original blank forms. I tried valiantly to fill in all of the correct information, but beyond my name and contact information, I was lost. I looked up the tooth number online, but had no way of knowing what the proper procedure codes should be. How was I to know which code number to assign filing a chipped tooth? I went back to the office in the middle of a workday to ask for the insurance codes, but found it dark and closed. However, the front door remained unlocked. I walked into the unlit lobby, picked up a piece of blank paper and wrote a note to the effect that I needed to know the exact amount I owed them (it was not clear from their paperwork) and would they *please* do me the favor of—just this once—inserting the correct procedure code and refiling with insurance? I left my stack of papers with the note on the front desk, thinking the matter would be handled. Boy, was I wrong!

Two days later, I received a certified letter at my front door. I signed for and opened the quite thick envelope. Inside was all of the paperwork I had left on their counter (including my handwritten note) along with a long typed letter from the dentist. The stern letter reiterated that they are not required to refile insurance forms, and that if I did not pay at once they would sue me for payment!?!?! The painful process had lasted so long that by now the bill was a few days overdue. Instead of inserting the correct procedure code and faxing the document to my insurance company (which would have been free of charge and have required, at most, 5 minutes of work), this dentist had taken at least 20 minutes to type me an angry letter, driven it to the post office, and paid them $1.50 to send me a certified letter. All of this in order to avoid helping a potential customer!

Stunned, I drove down to the dentist's office with the paperwork in hand and asked the hygienist if she would please give me the correct insurance code and inform me of the exact amount I owed them so I could write them a check and be out of their lives forever. When the dentist recognized me, his eyes grew wide and he began to shout at me, "I want you out of my office! Get out of my office! You are the worst patient I have ever had in my career!" I replied that I had come to pay, yet he continued to scream, "You write that check and then get out of my office! I never want to see you in here again!"

Once the assistant had provided me with the correct amount I wrote the check but waited to give it to her until she had written the proper insurance codes on my paperwork and returned them to me. I left, never to return. To this day, I still shake my head in disbelief at the dentist's bizarre actions. Is he utterly unaware that a single disgruntled patient today wields enormous power to devastate a business via online reviews, and that such reviews may linger near the tops of search engines for years? And can be easily found and read in mere seconds by almost anyone in the world? And that residents of my town will almost certainly seek out those reviews? Why would he choose to alienate me, and to do so viciously?

I reflected on the bizarre experience and briefly flirted with the idea of issuing a retaliatory stab to the heart of his practice by writing up the whole fiasco on Yelp! Instead, I wrote the dentist a letter. It is printed below:

Dear Dr. Xxxxxx,

My recent encounter with your practice left me upset enough to write (for the first time in my life) a scathing online review that would have certainly cost you many times the monetary price I paid for your services a few weeks ago. However, I've chosen not to do that. Instead of writing an online review, I decided to constructively put in writing my thoughts for your eyes only. These comments are intended to help, not hurt, and I hope that you will receive them in that spirit. If you take my comments to heart, they will make you many, many thousands of dollars in the future. Should you reject them, it will probably cost you a small fortune as other less well-intentioned patients have similarly unpleasant interactions with your practice and choose to publicly air their frustrations via online forums. Keep in mind that for every customer that complains, there are usually many more who harbored the same complaint but never expressed it to you. Instead, they simply voted with their feet and quietly took their business elsewhere. And in many cases, they told everyone except you of their dissatisfaction.

I found you to be professionally competent and knowledgeable. However, your chairside manner is a bit brusque. I knew shortly after meeting you that while I might be happy to have you for my dentist, my wife would insist on someone kinder, gentler, and friendlier. I knew when I left your office that day that I would be unlikely to return, even though you performed the requested service well. I would prefer that my whole family use the same dentist, whomever that might turn out to be.

Please be constantly aware that your patients (even highly educated ones) are unqualified to evaluate your clinical skills. We usually have no idea what you're doing inside our mouths. We hear clinking, smell strange odors, feel scraping, and see the top ends of instruments protruding from our mouths. But we don't know whether you are executing the required dental procedures well or not. Hours, days and weeks later we know whether our condition is better, but we have no way of knowing whether a different dentist might have caused more (or less) pain or shortened (or lengthened) our convalescence or had greater (or lesser) success. We sometimes can't even know for sure whether we would have gotten better with no trip to the dentist at all. <u>We can only judge you by your chairside manner</u>, so that's what we *do. It may seem unfair, but this is a largely unchangeable fact. That is how most of your patients will decide whether to return or not, regardless of your clinical skills.*

On my one and only visit (as a patient) to your clinic, I inadvertently provided you with my Humana health insurance card instead of my Humana dental card. It was an innocent mistake, as they look identical when I'm not wearing my reading glasses. When the insurance denied my claim, I quickly realized my mistake and called to provide you with the correct policy number. Your assistant replied that you are "not required" (you would later use that same word) to file insurance claims twice. While I'm confident that you are technically correct, no one was implying that you are <u>legally</u> bound to do so. You are, however, required by the realities of the marketplace to make doing business with you as smooth, friendly, and easy as possible. Instead, you made it an excruciating chore, and then refused to help me even by providing the proper insurance code for filing a chipped tooth. Had I been inclined to return to your practice, this lack of helpfulness alone would have driven me and my family (and our healthcare dollars) into the arms of another dentist. Your hygienist's response should have been, "As a rule, we don't typically re-file *denied insurance claims, but we're happy to help out this time."*

Instead, when I merely asked for help filling out the technical aspects of the insurance form, you threatened to sue me?!?!?! Wouldn't it have been better (and quicker, cheaper and more constructive) to pick up the phone and have a conversation with me than to take the time to write a long letter and send it via certified mail? As a rule, I encourage you to put only <u>positive</u> comments in writing. When you offend someone via the written word, the recipient will likely read it over and over again and stew over it and become angrier with each reading. They will tend to read between the lines and assign the most reprehensible motives and character flaws to the writer. When negative interactions are needed (and these must be avoided with patients whenever possible), they must be conducted in a telephone or in-person conversation (hopefully the latter) so that you will have the opportunity to instantly sense the patient's reaction and to quickly mitigate any negative emotions by offering explanatory comments. Your smile and compassionate tone of voice will thus soften the blow, and hopefully save the patient's business.

In conclusion, let me just remind you that I and my family had just moved to Dripping

Springs and were in need of a new dentist. We are exactly the type of patient every practice wants and needs: we are honest, clean and polite. We take our dental health seriously and we always pay our bills. You never had to spend a penny marketing to get me through your door; I just walked in because you were the closest dentist to my new home. We were all ripe for the picking to become your loyal patients (and even advocates) for years to come. But you instead repeatedly engaged in behaviors that alienated me almost from the moment I first sat in your chair up until the current day. Such behavior is suicidal for a business.

I genuinely wish you well in your practice, and have no plans to air my grievance with you in any other forum.

Sincerely,

Billy Riggs

I believe it was a good letter, but I never sent it. My wife feared that the man might come burn our house down or kill us. I doubt that is the case, but one can never be too careful. I recently noticed that this dentist's office now stands empty and is available for lease. No surprise there. In light of the incredible staying power of online interviews, the wise businessperson will redouble efforts to exceed the customer's expectations.

Exercise Questions:

1. As a group, read some of your online reviews.

2. If there are negative reviews, should you respond to them online directly, or change your procedures to prevent the problem from occurring again?

3. Can you design a strategy to encourage happy customers to leave online reviews that will help overwhelm and drown out existing negative ones?

4. What can be done to help satisfy a frustrated customer before they can write a negative review?

Chapter 15

GOOD ISN'T
GOOD ENOUGH

One of the grandest illusions clouding the topic of customer service is this: good service will be rewarded. This seemingly obvious truism is actually false, a misconception. Good service, in reality, is the *norm*. It is expected and quickly forgotten. When I enter a convenience store to purchase a Diet Dr. Pepper, I hand the clerk $1.29 and he hands me the drink. I depart feeling no sense of indebtedness to the clerk, just as he feels no sentimental twinge of gratitude toward me. To be sure, I'm glad the store is there and stocked with Diet Dr. Pepper, and the owner (though perhaps not the clerk) is happy people like me come in regularly to purchase their products. Nevertheless, the event is utterly forgettable because the transaction was entirely devoid of the two critical factors mentioned in Chapter 9: relationship and emotion. On the contrary, it was nothing more than an even-steven trade, and 5 minutes later neither of us can even remember what the other looks like. The vast majority of business interactions are of this variety, and *they do not impress customers positively*; they merely avoid affecting them negatively. It is not enough to merely avoid angering or frustrating the customer, which would be merely to institutionalize mediocrity. It is not even enough to satisfy him or her. One must go a step further to delight, amaze, and dazzle the customer. You must make the customer feel that doing business with you was a wonderful experience.

An entire industry thrives around delivering customer satisfaction. Yet, satisfaction doesn't win you any brownie points. To be sure, a customer that is dissatisfied is unlikely to return unless you have something else going for you, like really low prices or a very convenient location. In a purely binary choice between satisfied customers and dissatisfied ones, the former is obviously better. But there is a third option: you can set yourself utterly apart from your competitors by *wowing* your customers. You can astonish them with kindness, cheerfulness and efficiency. You can dazzle them by doing more than is expected or by delivering your product or service with a flair. The goal must be far higher than just satisfying patrons, for no one walks away from such an encounter and eagerly calls a friend to recount the story of how they were "satisfied" with their experience. Not just customer satisfaction, but customer *satis-passion* is your goal, in which customers' positive emotions are engaged and then unleashed as free advertising on the world. Your business should strive to become the type of place others seek to visit even if they don't normally buy your product or service. It's almost a tourist attraction. You want those who do business with you to be *blown away*.

Years ago I was invited to be the luncheon speaker for a convention on Hilton Head Island, South Carolina. In those days, before the completion of a major highway, Hilton Head was a 50-minute drive down serpentine back roads through the bayou of South Carolina from the nearest major airport in Savannah, Georgia. My schedule required that I fly into Savannah late Friday evening, and I was hesitant to make that long drive down unfamiliar roads in the dark. I elected, instead, to find a motel near the Savannah airport, spend the night there, and make the drive over to the speech venue after daybreak the following morning. I went online and found a cheap motel (my client was on a very tight budget) near the Savannah airport, and even went to the extreme of prepaying the non-refundable rate to lock in the lowest possible charge for my customer. I arrived on-schedule in Savannah at about 10:00 p.m., rented my car, and drove to the motel. It was closed! Note that it was not closed *down*, it was merely locked up for the night. A sign on the door explained that the office closed at 10:00 p.m. and would reopen at 5:00 a.m!??! Thus, I was standing in the dark with a prepaid receipt in my hand for a room I couldn't use. I was fit to be tied. I drove to a nearby gas station and asked for advice. The clerk recommended that I try the Fairfield Marriott hotel, which was also near the Savannah airport. I drove there and found, of course, that it was open 24/7. The lady behind the registration desk was pleasant and efficient. The check-in process was smooth. The room was clean and comfortable. The continental breakfast the next morning was fresh and tasty. My entire experience at the Fairfield Marriott was a good one. I drove to Hilton Head, delivered my speech, then headed back to Savannah for my flight home. It was during that flight that I made a resolution in my heart. I resolved that if ever I returned to Savannah, I would stay... *where*? It's not what you think. I didn't decide that I would return to the Fairfield Marriott, though they were certainly good. Instead, I resolved to stay *anywhere but that first motel!* In fact, I have returned to Savannah at least half-a-dozen times since then and I've yet to return to the Fairfield Marriott.

You may wonder, "Why wouldn't you just stay at the Fairfield Marriott? They were good!" Here's the answer that lurks (though unspoken and perhaps unconsciously) in the mind of every customer:

because it's also good at most other places! Service is also good at the Hampton Inn, the Drury, La Quinta, the Courtyard Marriott, the Hilton, the Hyatt, the Wyndham, and the Westin. It's usually good at the Holiday Inn or the Best Western, too. And *if it's good almost everywhere, being good isn't good enough*. If it's good everywhere, I'm going to choose the place with the lowest price or the most convenient location. To succeed, you have to be better than good. In fact, you have to be so much better that you make an unforgettable impression on the customer that lingers in the memory and makes people want to tell others of their experience. Here is a hard, cold dose of reality: good customer service doesn't create customer loyalty. It just prevents hostility. Good customer service is no longer much of a competitive advantage; it is the price of entry into the marketplace. Good customer service is the norm. It is expected and it will be immediately forgotten. There are only two types of customer service that people remember and respond to: fabulous and bad. Everything in between disappears down the memory hole within a few minutes. The only customer service experiences you tend to remember are those with people you know or those that evoke *emotions*, whether good ones or bad ones.

GOOD CUSTOMER SERVICE DOESN'T
CREATE CUSTOMER LOYALTY;
IT JUST PREVENTS HOSTILITY.

During my speeches on customer service, I frequently ask audience members to raise their hands if they've eaten at a new restaurant (new to them, I mean) in the past few weeks at which they determined the service to be "good." About a fourth of the audience typically responds affirmatively. I then instruct them to leave their hands in the air if they now regard themselves as loyal customers of that restaurant. Almost every hand immediately goes down, proving my point: good customer service is rarely rewarded. Customers respond to service that wows them, whether positively or negatively. Everything in between is forgotten. There are several ways in which you can make them say, "Wow! That was fabulous!"

Commit to Solving the Client's Problem

All great customer service is a problem-solving endeavor. Whether the customer needs a piece of artwork to adorn a blank wall, a lawnmower to replace a broken-down one, a home near better schools, or a car big enough for the new twins, or a clearer explanation of health insurance benefits, a great service provider is first and foremost a problem solver. Customers fall in love with companies that solve their problems quickly and effectively. Clients are wowed when they consistently enter with a problem and leave with a solution. Service providers must be tenacious in dealing with every customer, no matter how long it takes, to resolve the issue that caused them to enter your store or call your company.

Though it sounds crazy, even sending customers to your competitors to solve their problems will probably bear positive fruit in the long run on those occasions you are unable to resolve their issue. Zappos (the online shoe retailer) does not ship shoes outside of the United States. However, when a customer requests this service, he or she is immediately referred to a list of companies that *do* offer overseas shipping. Even though Zappos loses the sale (that they weren't going to get anyway), they may actually win the customer in the long run. Customers know that when they call Zappos, their problem will be solved or their question answered before they hang up the phone. This can be a huge incentive for a prospect to go to Zappos first every time they need shoes.

Use names

Some of the best pieces of advice I ever received came from a man who died before I was born. Dale Carnegie wrote his perennial bestseller, *How to Win Friends and Influence People*, in 1936 and I somehow came across it and read it as a sophomore in high school. It is an easy read describing simple practices that cause people to like and trust you. I was somewhat of an outcast before I read the book, but three years later—by applying the principles in this classic book—I was elected president of my college's freshman class.

Carnegie states, "Remember that a person's name is to that person the sweetest and most important sound in any language." Memorizing and using people's names makes them feel special and important. Conversely, not knowing the name of a person you've met several times makes them feel that you deem them unimportant and utterly forgettable, that they just blend into the background in your eyes. Using someone's name, however, must not be overdone to the degree that the focus is on your remarkable memory, not your new friend. Artificially ramming someone's name into a sentence doesn't say, "You're special," but "I'm a used car salesman trying to manipulate you." In fact, a study I read recently concluded that using a customer's name more than 4 times in an encounter actually *decreases* sales.

By the time I arrived on my college campus as a 17 (almost 18) year old young man, I had worked diligently on this principle. I obtained the college annual from the previous year from the library and memorized the names of all of the upperclassmen so that I was often able to greet them by name before we'd even met. I secretly wrote down the names of my fellow freshmen after I met them and later would repeat their names over and over in my mind as I pictured them. Before I went to class, I would mentally review the identities of the other students in each class so that I could immediately greet them by name when I entered the room rather than groping strenuously to recall them on the spot. The result is that people felt that I noticed them and cared about them (which I did, by the way).

For the past several years, the top-rated hotel in the Chicago area has been The Langham. Their customer service is legendary, and one of the reasons lies in the fact that employees are expected to learn the names of the guests and to call them by name when they pass in the hallways, serve them in the restaurants, or interact with them at the front desk. Using a person's name after you've only met them once is magical! It makes them say, "Wow! I'm not just a number or a revenue source. I'm a human being."

Model Service from the Top Down

I recently spoke at the brand new Hotel ZaZa just outside Houston, Texas. It's a boutique hotel chain that currently operates two hotels in the Houston area and one in Dallas, with construction underway for a fourth in Austin. The day I arrived marked the one-week anniversary of the hotel's opening so the facility was immaculate. No surprise there. What was shocking, however, was the cheerful, competent, friendly staff that operated with efficiency as though they had been in business for a decade. Valets not only delivered my car in two or three minutes flat, they greeted me with a smile. The check-in process was smooth. Bellmen came promptly when called and housemen had the stage all ready for my evening presentation before I arrived, which was 10 hours before my speech! But the most salient feature they shared was their friendliness. All of them acted like they'd known me for years.

As I departed the hotel the following morning, I came out of the elevator and was momentarily confused as to whether I should turn right or left to find the exit. Immediately, a smiling man to my right (who was dressed in such a way that I couldn't tell whether he was an employee or another guest) said, "Looking for the front door?" I nodded. "Right this way," he said, gesturing with his right hand. With that, he proceeded to walk me to the front door and ask me how I had enjoyed my stay. He handed me his business card saying, "If you ever need anything at any of our hotels, give me a call." I looked at the business card as best I could without my glasses on, and couldn't make out his name. But I *could* make out the word, "President." I said, "You're the president of the company?" "Man of the people," he joked. I couldn't resist taking the opportunity to tell him how brilliant their service had been, especially for a property that had been open only 7 days, and he told me his secret.

"We want to be your best friend when you're on the road," he stated. I asked, "But how do you get them to be so consistently friendly?" His reply was, "We only hire people who are naturally friendly, cheerful and outgoing. We can teach people to answer the phone, carry bags, park cars, and check people into the correct rooms, but you can't teach friendliness." Deeply embedding the concept of The Magic Touch into your company requires that managers model the behavior they want their frontline staff to demonstrate. If leaders quietly retire to their ivory towers and become progressively more remote from customers, frontline staff members will unconsciously assume that desk work is more important than customer interactions and behave accordingly.

Work Hard to Please Customers

Work ethic, in any endeavor, is often the difference between failure and success, and customer service is no different. I have a colleague who routinely allows details to "take care of themselves," and he's always shocked when they don't. Typos, scheduling snafus, missed appointments, and overlooked items are the norm with him, and I know why. It's because he doesn't spend time combing through every conceivable detail of a project as he should. Taking an extra 3 minutes to run spell-check, or to make a checklist and check it twice, or take inventory of everything in his briefcase before leaving home in the morning, or review his calendar the night before would solve the vast majority of the problems he faces (and creates for others!), but he's simply unwilling to make that effort. I can only imagine the frustration that his clients must experience right up until the day they stop doing business with him.

Another friend of mine is currently searching for a new home. He's retired and wealthy and hired a realtor to help him find his dream home. The realtor was given a budget of up to a million dollars for a home of about 2000 square feet (he and his wife don't want a huge house to clean and maintain) with a spectacular view located within 20 minutes of downtown Austin. My friend recently remarked to me that *the realtor is of no help whatsoever.* The supposed "sales professional" recently sent him links to half-a-dozen homes, none of which fit the three simple criteria or even came close. My friend—in under 30 minutes—easily found a few homes that met his specifications by merely doing an internet search. The realtor was obviously not trying to serve his customer, but just scattering buckshot in hopes of grazing an acceptable target. Needless to say, the realtor was replaced by another who doesn't mind spending the time and effort it takes to meet his customers' needs.

Be Proactive

Good customer service usually occurs reactively. There are times when you must wait for a customer to ask a question or express a need before responding to it in dazzling fashion. However, *great* customer service is often proactive. There is a huge perceived difference between being nice to someone whenever you happen to see them versus calling them on the phone to see how they are doing. You would be foolish to wait for your significant other to become offended at your thoughtlessness after your forget a birthday or an anniversary. Instead, you should constantly be thinking of them and their needs and plan activities that will please them and remind them of how important they are to you. Likewise, great customer service sometimes involves thinking of your best customers and anticipating their needs. It involves calling them on the phone to remind them of a sale on their favorite brand of shirt, or sending them a card on their birthday, or holding back an item that you're sure they would like, or forwarding a link to a trip they might enjoy. It means calling them first when their desired item arrives on the truck so they'll have the first opportunity to come pick it up.

Such service requires that employees actively strive to remember the particular likes and dislikes of customers and to recall details of conversations that could easily be forgotten. The wise service provider will write down the names and interests of particular customers and review them from time to time to refresh his or her memory.

Set High Expectations

Customer service isn't created by companies; it's delivered by individuals. The myriad of positive touches required to evoke wows is delivered not by a business, but by conscientious employees one at a time. Companies should create and nurture systems that make it easy for staff members to spot and meet customers' needs, and to reward them when they do, but ultimately service is provided by people, not institutions or organizations. Only when enough of your staff members dedicate themselves to routinely exceeding expectations is customer service transformed into a memorable experience. For this reason, the dream of dazzling customers must be injected into the soul of each staff member. Managers must set themselves on fire with a passion to produce stellar service, one that burns so brightly that those close by can't help but ignite, as well. They then become evangelists for your company rather than mere employees.

Patrons who have been wowed usually rave about the service provided by a particular person in a company, not the company as a whole. Companies can train their people to provide such service, they can liberate their people to make good decisions, they can create a culture in which great service is the norm, but ultimately it is the individual employee that provides the wow moments to which customers respond. They do this only when they have caught the vision of The Magic Touch. Starbucks CEO Howard Schultz wrote in his book, *Onward*, that his employees "are the true ambassadors of our brand, the real merchants of romance and theater, and as such the primary catalysts for delighting customers." If you can cause employees to buy into the vision of the entire company and feel that they are an important, even if tiny, part of fulfilling an important mission, they will naturally raise their performance and seek to wow customers. This is a goal that could never be achieved by an internet ad, a billboard, or a television commercial.

Be Consistent

There's an adage that circulates in the restaurant business: "You're only as good as your last meal." I can tell you from experience that it's true. I've always liked the hamburgers at Fuddruckers. But the last time I went there almost a year ago, my burger wasn't nearly up to par. It was downright plain and dry, and I haven't been back since. They'll never know that I stopped patronizing their business, or why (unless they read this book). I simply vanished and took my money with me. There's no doubt that I'm not really being fair to the good people at Fuddruckers. Maybe the cook called in sick that day and the grill was being manned by a rookie. Maybe the supplier failed them by delivering a poor quality of beef that week. Or maybe mine was just a single bad burger on a day when they served hundreds of excellent ones. But I can't help it. The thought of going to Fuddruckers just doesn't excite me any longer. When my wife asks, "Where do you want to eat tonight?" I don't bring up Fuddruckers like I used to. Sadly, the last taste left in my mouth is the one that remains.

Presumably, the same principle holds true in any profession, not just food service. I am only as marketable a motivational speaker as the last speech a given person heard me deliver. If I bomb at a convention, anyone in the audience who was considering booking me for their next event scratches me from the list, regardless of how many home runs I might have hit in the past. A tailor is only as good as the last garment he or she altered. Any goodwill built up over years might easily be swept away by a single shoddy job, unless they quickly step into service recovery mode as described in Chapter 5.

This helps us understand why every employee must be fully committed to the mission of providing mind-boggling customer service. A single wow-producing act of service by a great employee might we easily wiped out by the mediocre or poor service inflicted by another. Whatever ground gained by an encounter with one staff member may well be overcome and undone by another. The only solution is to create a culture that demands over-the-top service from every employee in every customer contact.

Improve Constantly

I'm not really a magician; I just play one onstage. I perform acts of apparent mind-reading, but they're just tricks. I can't actually predict the future, though it seems to my audiences I can. Nevertheless, I'm going to hazard a guess about your future. I predict that if you provide excellent service to your customers, and keep it up at that exact level for ten years, in one decade you will be mediocre, and in two decades, you will be obsolete or out of business. That's a tough word to hear, but I'm convinced it's true, because service that is considered stellar today ten years from now will be old hat, and ten years later completely unacceptable. This is why you must continually improve. You have to get better every year just to stay where you currently are relative to the competition.

I'm old enough to remember what it was like to stay in a hotel 35 years ago. In the 70s, hotels — even nice ones — didn't have irons and ironing boards in the rooms. If you wanted to iron your shirt, you had to call the front desk to reserve *the* iron. You would then have to go down to the front desk to borrow it. The employee would hand you a tiny ironing board (about three feet long) with the iron. You would then take it to your room, fold out the little two-inch legs and place it on your bed. You would then wet a towel to try to remove the gunk left on the iron by the last 300 guests, iron your shirt, then return everything to the front desk within 30 minutes for use by the next guest. Today, however, even cheap hotels offer irons and full-size ironing boards in every room! In the eighties even nice hotels didn't have hair dryers in the rooms. (Back then, I needed one!) Now, almost all hotels provide hair dryers in nice little carry bags. Hotels used to provide one tiny bar of soap and one bottle of blended shampoo and conditioner. Now they have facial soap, bath soap (with convenient little bumps on them to create a massage effect!), shampoo, conditioner, lotion and shower caps. Recently, they've started putting Keurig coffeemakers in every room so you can choose the type of coffee you want. Even excellent hotels that did not improve are now out of business, because the bar rises every single year. What is accepted as great service today will soon be considered average, and eventually rendered obsolete.

Innovate

One of the most effective ways to wow a customer is to provide a service or product that was previously unknown. There was, of course, a day in which the telephone was unheard of. Once a person had spoken with a distant friend through one, however, it would be inconceivable that they would not react by saying, "Wow!" Each time a new par-adigm is created via innovation, the potential for a new wow-making moment is ushered in along with it. For this reason, the wise will always be on the lookout for ways to create or, at least, to capitalize on new waves of innovation.

At its height, Blockbuster Video had over 9000 stores scattered all over North America. Every Friday afternoon their parking lots would be jammed with the automobiles of people who were wandering their aisles in search for just the right titles to bring home for movie night. Today, almost none of their stores remains. Empty slots in strip malls serve as a reminder of how success can become its own greatest enemy. Blockbuster morphed easily and seamlessly from films on Beta cassettes into exclusively those in VHS for-mat. They flirted briefly with video discs the size of old LP albums, but discarded them when the market never developed. They then progressed fluidly into DVDs when cassettes became obso-lete. Each development represented a small change within the existing paradigm which required cus-tomers to come to a store during business hours, pick out what they wanted, and take it home with them. Red Box then set up vending machines that allowed such rentals around the clock. Netflix later began mailing DVDs directly to customers in their homes, offering to mail their next movie as soon as the first one was returned. Blockbuster weath-ered each of these storms, for the newer modalities altered the original paradigm only in the manner, availability, or speed of the delivery. But Blockbuster management was completely blindsided by a tectonic shift in the market to a totally new paradigm: on-demand streaming video. Not that they weren't warned, mind you.

In 2000, Netflix approached Blockbuster and offered to sell their newfangled, thus far unprofitable, streaming company to them for $50 million, which represented a mere 1% of total revenues for the behemoth Blockbuster company that year. The Blockbuster CEO, John Antioco, didn't warm to the idea and replied, "No thanks." He couldn't see the potential of the streaming video market, and one can hardly blame him. When your entire day is spent trying to create better and faster ways to distribute physical DVDs and videocassettes, it's difficult to envision the next huge jump in technology. Being a genius about renting DVDs doesn't prepare one at all to deliver digital content over the internet, does it? To the contrary, it runs the risk of setting you up to laugh it off.

Today, Netflix is worth over 90 Billion Dollars, which is 1800 times more than the offered sale price. Within 11 years of declining to buy Netflix, Blockbuster was bankrupt. Today, its stock is worth less than half-a-penny. Netflix, by contrast, has seen their stock rise to over $275 per share, a 13,000% increase. It's hard to see the next wave of an industry coming when you're in the middle of the current one. But it's not impossible.

Netflix has, thus far, not repeated Blockbuster's mistake. They shifted their emphasis from mailing hard DVDs to streaming movies online. Now, they have moved even further to produce their own original films and television series available only to their subscribers. No one knows what the next wave will (or even could) be, but Netflix has thus far proven that they can make the jump to the new paradigm. It is difficult to anticipate a new paradigm when you are engrossed in an existing one. This is why you must strive to hire people who are on the cutting edge of new ones who might open your eyes to the next wave.

Seize the Day

In some professions, opportunities to impress customers are rare. Insurance is one. After one buys an auto or homeowners insurance policy, there is little interaction between the agent and the policyholder, save a few bills and newsletters. When a claim is filed, however, this is when the agent must leap into action to earn his paycheck. Otherwise, if you never have to file a claim, the cheapest policy is, by definition, the best. Every filed claim is an opportunity to prove that the customer's trust was well-placed and to win that same customer's loyalty for the future.

Encounters with doctors, lawyers, funeral directors and law enforcement personnel also take place under negative circumstances. Customers don't like to deal with people in these professions and do so only when they must. Consequently, interactions are rare, making the need to dazzle even more important. Just as every ball possession in the fourth quarter of a football game gains increased importance (since there are so few of them left), every encounter with a customer is elevated in importance precisely because they are so infrequent. While one might have hundreds of interactions with an airline, a department store, or a grocery outlet customer touches in the fields described above might be quite few. Every opportunity to win over customers must be seized because the next chance to do so might be years away.

Conclusion:

Franz Mesmer (1734-1815) was a German doctor who believed that the planets and stars affected the human body and played a mysterious role in causing or healing diseases. He called those mystical effects, "mesmerism." The term today refers to hypnotism and describes one who is entranced, under the influence of another person in a way that leaves them transfixed and pliable. A person in such a state of unexpected bewilderment today is referred to as "mesmerized." This is the effect evoked by those who provide "magical" customer service. This book is the attempt of a magician and showman to help readers raise the bar from customer service that merely satisfies, to that which dazzles, enchants, captivates, and enthralls. Now it's up to you. It's *showtime*!

About the Author

Billy Riggs has been called "The Dr. Phil of Magic," and is America's source for all things attitude! Through books, recordings, and live keynote speeches Billy uses an unusual blend of comedy, music, magic, and motivation to spread his positive attitude to millions of people on five continents. A spellbinding communicator, Mr. Riggs honed his uplifting message and speaking skills in the pulpit, founding one of America's fastest-growing churches at the age of 29. Though his presentations now are secular, audiences sometimes sense the old preacher in him, stirred by his sincerity and power on the platform. In 2002, Mr. Riggs was presented the highest earned award of the National Speakers Association: the Certified Speaking Professional, or CSP. Since

1995, he has breathed The Magic of Attitude into people, companies, and organizations.

<u>But the goose bumps aren't always the result of dramatic oratory!</u> When Billy Riggs appears, things on stage begin to disappear! Using world-class magical illusions to drive his points home, Billy's presentations have transformed hundreds of otherwise ordinary conferences into something truly special. His quick wit and quicker hands spread laughter and raise morale as listeners learn to reshape their destinies by eliminating their "Grand Illusions" and embracing even grander truths.

Billy Riggs lives in Austin, Texas with his wife and son.

Billy Riggs Speaks at Conferences

Master *DIS*-illusionist!

If you enjoyed this book, you'll *love* hearing Billy in person! When his powerful message is combined with magic and comedy, the result is a keynote that is a rollercoaster of laughter, inspiration and learning. Businesses, associations, chambers of commerce, school districts, government agencies, and charities have all proclaimed his programs as the best they've ever experienced. With 30 years performing on 5 continents and 12 cruise ships, he has experience you can trust.

Available programs include:

Positively Magical Selling!	for salespeople
How to Achieve the Impossible!	for managers
The Power of a P.M.A.	for everyone
Positively Magical Service!	for service providers
The Magic of Network Marketing!	for MLMs
Beyond Belief!	for youth

As seen on PBS!

Billy Riggs, Master *DIS*-illusionist!
www.billyriggs.com